SUPPORTING PUPILS WITH EMOTIONAL DIFFICULTIES

Creating a Caring Environment for All

ROB LONG AND JONATHAN FOGELL

David Fulton Publishers
London

David Fulton Publishers Ltd
Ormond House, 26–27 Boswell Street, London WC1N 3JD
http://www.fultonbooks.co.uk

First published in Great Britain in 1999 by David Fulton Publishers
Reprinted 2000

Note: The rights of Rob Long and Jonathan Fogell to be identified as the authors of this work has been asserted by them in accordance with the Copyright, Designs and Patents Act 1988.

Copyright © Rob Long and Jonathan Fogell 1999

British Library Cataloguing in Publication Data
A catalogue record for this book is available from the British Library

ISBN 1–85346–595–X

Typeset by Textype Typesetters, Cambridge
Printed in Great Britain by Bell and Bain Ltd, Glasgow

Contents

1 Emotional Development: Context and Relevance

Over many years of educational debate, the efforts of government and professionals to define the role of education and to make it more relevant to the twenty-first century have been gaining momentum. The recent pace was set in the Great (educational) Debate, launched by the then Prime Minister, James Callaghan, in 1977. For most children, the business of schooling has continued despite this controversy with relatively few complications. Schools have continued their core business of developing well-adjusted young people fit to take their place in the world. In so doing, schools provide their pupils with a unique set of indelible memories and values, some not so good but mostly good.

For some children at the margins, however, school life can be fraught with complications. These complications are often thrust upon the child by others. Sometimes they are generated by the child's response to his or her environment. For such children, despite an unceasing flow of educational innovations and sometimes re-inventions, there has been continuing evidence of growing dissatisfaction and disillusionment with schooling. This is seen through the increasing rate of exclusion and truancy from our schools.

While the number of pupils excluded from schools still remains small in relation to the overall school population it has risen sharply in recent years.

- 4,000 permanent exclusions occurred in 1991–92. The figures were collected voluntarily and so are probably underestimated for this year.
- The number of permanent exclusions (recorded more reliably) was 13,500+ in 1996/97 (Godfrey and Parsons 1998).
- In addition to the rising rate of permanent exclusion the rate of temporary exclusions was running at approximately 135,000 per year in 1996/7 (Smith 1998).

There was a slowdown in the general rate of increase in exclusions in 1996/97 but the trend in special and primary schools continued upwards.

Recent evidence (Godfrey and Parsons 1998, Cabinet Office 1998) suggests the following reasons for the increase in exclusions:

- high levels of family stress;
- poor acquisition of basic skills, particularly literacy;
- limited aspirations and opportunities;
- poverty;
- poor relationships with pupils, parents or teachers.

All of these factors are interwoven with the emotional well-being of the child, the school's potential to create an emotionally supportive ethos and the capacity of families and communities to create stable environments for children.

Whatever the background to an exclusion from school, the pupil affected is likely to be at a considerable disadvantage. Evidence indicates that excluded pupils 'are relegated to the margins of society while teachers find it difficult to cope, and the public picks up the cost for children who drift onto the streets without qualifications and skills where they can easily gravitate towards crime and prison' (Smith 1998).

It has been argued, notably by some teacher professional organisations, that if certain pupils are not excluded other children can be at a considerable disadvantage. Such arguments emphasise the teacher's right to teach and the pupils' right to learn. After all, the behaviours cited for exclusion, if unchecked, are likely to adversely affect the prospects of students who behave appropriately. Reasons for exclusion often include:

- bullying, fighting and assaults on peers;
- disruption, misconduct and unacceptable behaviour;
- verbal abuse to peers;
- verbal abuse to staff;
- theft;
- defiance and disobedience;
- drugs (smoking, alcohol, cannabis);
- vandalism and arson;
- physical abuse and assault on staff.

The argument at its simplest would suggest that there is a need for schools to make explicit behavioural boundaries and the conditions that will result in a pupil being excluded. By implementing these and then making adequate provision for those excluded in the form of special schools or units, schools could get on with the task of teaching those children who want to learn.

The issues around exclusions are complicated and are therefore likely to require complex solutions. The central problem with the use of exclusions as a sanction is the apparent arbitrary nature of its usage. A number of groups are disproportionately likely to be excluded: children with special needs; African-Caribbean children; and children in care. Of excluded pupils 83 per cent are boys; 80 per cent are between 12 and 15 and half are 14 or 15. Exclusion rates vary greatly from school to school, but tend to be higher in areas of social deprivation.

> Some schools are so anxious to avoid exclusions that they incur some danger to themselves as institutions, to staff and pupils. Others are only too ready to exclude. A few irresponsibly profligate in the use made of exclusion, devaluing it as a sanction (OFSTED 1997).

It seems that, from OFSTED's perspective at least, teachers are damned if they do and damned if they don't.

Moreover, one outcome of exclusion is to place further pressure on a vulnerable family, potentially hastening the need for Social Services Department or other Agency involvement. Thus the problem is not so much solved as shifted elsewhere.

The evidence that our society is becoming more complex for children is compelling. Burghes (1994) points to the rapid growth in the number of one-parent families. Amongst her conclusions she states that there are 'marked differences and poorer average outcomes are found for children from families disrupted by separation and divorce compared with those intact families'. Cockett and Tripp (1994) report that children whose families undergo a series of disruptions and changes are more likely to experience social, educational and health problems than those who remain intact. The message from these and many other reports appears to be that children can achieve stability and sound emotional growth within a range of family structures but the risk of emotional damage increases when the following factors or a combination of them exist:

- domestic conflict;
- poverty;

- inconsistent parenting;
- violence;
- abuse;
- poor housing;
- recent traumatic incident;
- time spent in care of SSD.

The Cabinet Office Social Exclusion Unit considered exclusions from school and truancy in one of their first investigations. Their report refers to the notion of 'joined-up thinking' that perceives problems and solutions from the variety of perspectives of the individual affected and the agencies working with them. The end result should be more creative solutions using the resources of a number of different agencies. The NHS thematic review *Nurturing Healthy Minds: Prevention and early intervention in child and adolescent mental health* promotes a similarly inclusive approach. They conclude that mental health in young people is indicated by the following:

- a capacity to enter into and sustain mutually satisfying personal relationships;
- continuing progression of psychological development;
- an ability to play and learn so that attainments are appropriate for age and intellectual level;
- a developing moral sense of right and wrong;
- the degree of psychological distress and maladaptive behaviour being within the normal limits for the child's age and context.

They advocate a future for supporting vulnerable children and young people that draws together Health, Education, Social Services Departments and Voluntary Agencies. They acknowledge a helpful start in the requirement for local authorities to produce joint Children's Services Plans to map-out local services from a range of different departments. This is a requirement of The Children Act (1989).

Many of the recent developments in education have been more concerned with mainstream issues. The focus has been on raising standards and increasing opportunities through the attainments of children. Whilst such an objective is laudable it is clear from the above discussion concerning exclusion and disaffection that the notion of attainments has been too narrow. The measurable standards, such as literacy and numeracy and examination results, tell only part of the story of a neighbourhood school's work. The next major challenge will be to find measures that recognise and celebrate the achievements of all children taking into account where they started from as much as where they end up.

The recent Green Paper *Excellence for All Children: Meeting Special Educational Needs* (DfEE 1997) and its subsequent action plan *Meeting Special Educational Needs: A Programme of Action* (DfEE 1998a) both acknowledge the complexities of work with children who present emotional and behavioural difficulties. The government set the following agenda in this area:

- the need for a national programme to help primary schools tackle the emotional behavioural difficulties at a very early stage;
- enhancing opportunities for all staff to improve their skills in teaching children with emotional and behavioural difficulties;
- supporting schools that cater for pupils with emotional and behavioural difficulties when they are experiencing problems;
- supporting young people with EBD at Key Stage 4.

Inevitably much of the focus has been on those pupils who present conduct-disorder behaviour. These statistically small groups of pupils often dominate the concerns of teachers because of the threat they pose to other pupils, to the social control of the school community, to the psychological well-being of the class teacher and, of course, to themselves. The groups of pupils who experience emotional difficulties are often of lesser concern to teachers and administrators. Yet these children may be showing the antecedents of greater problems later on. This is recognised in the DfEE Circular 1/98 *Behaviour Support Plans* (DfEE 1998b).

> The legal requirement to produce behaviour support plans focuses on pupils with behavioural difficulties. However, behavioural difficulties can frequently stem from emotional difficulties so pupils with emotional difficulties are identified as one of the vulnerable groups. Some services which provide for pupils with behavioural difficulties – in mainstream schools or other settings – would be likely to include pupils who have so far only experienced emotional difficulties, as well as pupils who have experienced behavioural difficulties or a combination of the two.

This book aims to explore the issues around the emotional development of children. It explores the considerations a teacher and school might have which follow from the question: How can we create a safe environment for all our pupils? The book deals with:

- recognising the importance of emotions to all within a school;
- the impact of emotions on a child's self-esteem and motivation;
- listening to children and helping them to help themselves;
- helping those children who have experienced particular difficulties;
- making sure the staffroom is respectful of teachers' emotions.

This book aims to give a positive message in the face of the difficulties described earlier. School can be a joyful place providing the best of memories and recollections for growing individuals. Teachers and allied professionals working in partnership with parents rightly take pride in the care and support they give to all children. In addition they give extra support to vulnerable children. Knowing that they have made a difference for the better in the life of a vulnerable child gives a sense of job satisfaction that is matched in few other professions.

Sometimes teachers need to look beyond their personal resources for ideas to help children with complex problems. They may also seek confirmation that they are following an appropriate strategy. This book is designed therefore as a support for the supporters. It concentrates on the primary school in the belief that laying firm foundations down for children enables them to cope better with the demands of secondary school and then life in general. The overall message of this book is encompassed in the old Irish proverb 'Get off to a good start and half your work is done' (Anon).

2 Making Sense of Emotions

The story of the Ghost with the Golden Leg

A teacher once took a party of school children on a canal-barge field trip. On the first night of the trip the teacher told the story of the Ghost with the Golden Leg. This is a very adaptable story, which can be converted to relate to the personal circumstances of the children who are listening.

It tells the story of a builder working many years ago. As he is digging the foundations of the building he comes across an old pirate's grave. The pirate had a false leg made of gold and was so afraid that his gold leg would be stolen from his grave that in his dying breath he put a curse on the leg. If anybody removed the leg from the grave the pirate would return from the dead to wreak revenge. Unfortunately the builder knows nothing of the curse and, not believing his good fortune, takes the leg home with him.

The story builds the audience up to a state of anticipation. When that anticipation is at a peak a prearranged clatter of falling cutlery or loud shriek from the back of the room interrupts the story and everybody jumps with fright. The teacher had first heard the story when he was a teenager on camp and had used it on many field trips since then. On this particular trip the story had the usual effect of making everybody jump and then break down into fits of giggles before all of the pupils assured one another that they were not really frightened and could see the ending coming a mile off!

After the field trip and back at school the teacher returned to the task of setting learning objectives for his pupils. One pupil, Peter, had particular reading difficulties. The teacher decided to use a behavioural objectives based phonics strategy. He carried out a baseline assessment using a criterion referenced test of phonic skills, and found that Peter could recognise only fifteen letters of the alphabet by name and sound.

Next he decided to use a programme of 'precision teaching' (Raybould and Solity 1982) and Peter received a daily dose of phonics to help him increase his knowledge of letter sounds and names. For two terms Peter had a fifteen-minute burst of instruction for five days of each week.

At the end of the summer term the teacher tested all of his pupils to see if they had made progress. He was pleased to note that Peter had mastered the skill of recognition of eighteen letters of the alphabet. After the summer holidays, one year after he had taken Peter on the barge trip, the teacher was planning to take his new class on a similar field adventure. On the first day of the new trip the teacher arrived in school and met Peter in the foyer. 'Oh,' said Peter, 'you are going on the barge today, aren't you?' 'Yes, but how do you know that?' replied the teacher. Peter gave his usual conspiratorial chuckle and pointed to the teacher's ex-Swedish Army sheepskin-lined coat. 'Because you are wearing your barge coat.'

Pleasantly impressed by this display of memory the teacher was astonished when Peter then said, 'Are you going to tell them the story of the Ghost with the Golden Leg?' 'Yes I probably will, Peter, so can you remember that story?' Needing no more invitation than that, Peter launched into a monologue which, though a little truncated, covered the essential points of the story.

Peter concluded by walking off down the corridor towards his classroom with an elaborate limp, wailing in a chilling ghostly voice 'I want my leg my goooolden leg!' This was a perfect imitation of the teacher telling the story which Simon had not heard for exactly one year.

Every teacher will have had a similar experience of a pupil who could learn facts and figures in one subject area, where motivation was high, whilst they floundered in another area.

This story is not related in an attempt to deny the value of behavioural approaches to teaching. Indeed as we move through the book we indicate that setting clear boundaries and expectations combined with a regard to the impact of rewards and sanctions are important features of creating a secure framework for a child. The story of Peter is aimed more at illustrating the strength and longevity of emotional experiences.

If the process of education is about transferring events, facts, relationships, insights and so on into our long term memory (LTM) it is important always to be mindful of LTM having two separate systems:

1. **Episodic memory** Often highly charged with emotional experiences, this is the memory associated with particularly strong experience and is often spurred into action by a piece of music, a turn of phrase, a smell, or a colour. Episodic memory plays a strong role in our conscious processing of new experiences by giving a reference point from which to compare and contrast new information.
2. **Semantic memory** Our mental filing system consists of all of the facts that we can recall in our knowledge base. Some of our semantic knowledge is difficult to access and only becomes readily usable with the help of *aides-mémoires*. Semantic memory is our wider knowledge which can be recalled (at some times more easily than others).

Knowledge can be stored for our lifetime, and it is knowledge that can help us change our emotions; for example, an awareness that a given snake is non-venomous can lesson our fear reaction to the snake. Indeed many of the later strategies described in this book are based on a firm belief that with time and effort children can learn to take control of their emotional responses. Unless we each learn this then there is always the possibility that emotions are lurking beneath the surface of our calm control and can take over in a flash.

Your conscious mind may be full up with lots of facts and figures and you suddenly hear a loud bang: your reaction to the loud bang will quickly push the facts and figures out of your consciousness. The same is not true conversely. Once the emotional brain clicks in it takes a protracted effort to displace fear with facts and to return to calmness.

Metaphors for emotions

Psychologists, sociologists, philosophers and a whole range of storytellers have tried to define emotions in a variety of ways. Many of the theoretical perspectives can be seen through the use of metaphors to explain emotions. No one metaphor will tell a complete story of emotions and the following list does not attempt to be definitive. Texts dealing with the psychological or biological theories of emotion (Strongman

1996, Cornelius 1996) will indicate that each perspective deals with emotion from the standpoint of the research methods used.

Indeed different perspectives working within the same paradigm may use similar metaphors to explain emotions. For example, the behaviourist psychologist may take a very different perspective from a biologist but essentially they use a similar metaphor, described here as the puppet metaphor, where the child's development of emotions is seen as a result primarily of external forces on the child. The following list should serve as a starting point for any group to explore the world of emotions. Each will be briefly considered to enable the reader to appreciate the complexity and variability as to how researchers have endeavoured to make sense of emotions.

Secrets and lies

Emotions are seen as something which can only be shared with those very close to the individual. In public at least one's emotions are a closely guarded secret.

Much emphasis has been placed in the past on denying the existence or being in full control of strong emotions. The ability to be dispassionate, objective, and scientific in relation to other human beings is a strong theme in Western culture. Psychologists showed this tradition when they sought to describe the people involved in their research as 'subjects'. The British Psychological Society has more recently deemed that 'participants' should replace the term 'subjects' (BPS 1993). This change in terminology reflects much more sensitivity to the impact of the investigation on the people being studied.

The emotional iceberg

The psychodynamic perspective of emotions is based on the notions of unconscious and conscious origins of our feelings. The actions of an individual are the result of their rational interpretation of feelings, which are related to a whole background of life experiences. Some of these feelings may be buried so deep that the individual cannot remember the circumstances which gave rise to them. The iceberg metaphor helps to explain the notion of the individual using a range of defence mechanisms to protect the core of their personality. The ego (essential identity) protects the individual from anxiety that may arise from:

- the primitive urges of the Id (the untrained animal instincts and drives);
- moral pressure from the super-ego (the source of high ideals);
- the reality of pain or danger;
- common defence mechanisms;
- displacement (choosing a substitute object for the expression of feelings because you cannot express them openly towards their real target);
- denial (refusing to acknowledge certain aspects of reality);
- rationalisation (finding an acceptable excuse for something which is really quite unacceptable, a 'cover-story' which preserves the self image of the individual or someone close to them).

Thus with the emotional iceberg metaphor what we see (and hear) is not necessarily what we get. The emotional experience is an interplay between the small amount of the individual we see above the surface and the huge complex substance of the individual which lies beneath the surface. Many would regard that which lies beneath the surface as the most dangerous part of the iceberg. Whether or not that is the case, it is clear that a full understanding of the iceberg can only be achieved by taking into account both its visible and hidden aspects.

The emotional puppet

This view of emotional development is predominant in behaviourist theories. Emotions are seen as simple visceral responses to external stimuli. The most important element of human behaviour is seen as what individuals do rather than what they think. The emphasis is therefore placed on the incidence of particular behaviours. This gives rise to the notion that the most important aspects of any behavioural incident are its antecedents, the nature of the behaviour itself and its consequences. Behaviour is seen as a complex pattern arising from variations on the theme of reward and sanction.

The puppet metaphor is also prevalent in biological explanations of emotions. Lewis and Samari (1985) describe the biological explanation of emotions as analogous to knee jerks or sneezes. They are unlearned, biologically controlled and subject to relatively little social influence.

The method actor

Emotions are a direct product of the scripts we construct when we interact with other human beings. The emotions we feel are a direct product of the role we are trying to perform and negotiate in social settings. The Social Constructionist Perspective embodies this metaphor. Strongman (1996) describes this perspective thus: 'For human adults they are internal and external stimuli that are interpreted, this interpretation mediating between the stimuli and any emotional response which might ensue. This means that any culture has its distinctive patterns of emotions that come from social practices'. This metaphor helps to explain why the expression of emotion on greeting and leaving people varies so much across different societies.

The building site

A Vygotsksian would emphasis the importance of cultural transfer in the development of emotions. Children are seen as having a range of skills and abilities to deal with life circumstances according to their stage of development. They also have a potential for growth and development that can be mediated by the adults around them. If the child learning to cope with his or her emotions is the building site, then adults can act as a support or scaffold whilst the child builds the necessary internal coping structure. In some ways Vygotsky reflected the secrets and lies metaphor. His concern was primarily higher order thinking skills which largely, and probably erroneously, precluded consideration of the impact of emotions on cognition.

The filter

Cognitive psychology and the more recent branch known as attribution theory see the emotions acting like a filter through which we pass new experiences. Rolls (1990) explored the relationship between emotion and its application to understanding the neural basis of cognition. He described eight functions of emotion.

1. The elicitation of automatic and endocrine responses which occur to facilitate the necessary actions following stimuli which have triggered emergency processes.
2. Behavioural responses as a consequence of affective evaluation of stimuli.
3. Motivation of organisms to seek positive and avoid negative stimuli.

4. Communication of emotional states which are important as a function of stability among social groups.
5. Social attachment which increases the survival probability of organisms belonging to the same species.
6. Attribution of survival value to positive and negative stimuli.
7. Influence in evaluation events or memories.
8. Influence in accessing stored memories.

The numbskull

Many years ago the children's comic *The Beezer* had a cartoon strip entitled 'The Numbskulls'. This told the tale of a group of people who had smaller people inhabiting their heads. The smaller people were the crew of the master vessel, the human. They observed the outside world and interpreted incoming signals and then gave the body instructions to act. I was never sure whether the Numbskulls were the full size humans or the little people that they had controlling their bodies. The image creates a very good metaphor for the biological theories of emotions. Here the body is seen as giving a visceral response to certain emotion-provoking stimuli.

The cookery book

Personality theorists would explain the emotional development of children with reference to the stable features of their personality and the relationship of personality traits to overt behaviour. The study of personality has tried to explain why we have a feeling of consistency of thought and values despite the fact that life presents us with situations which vary enormously. Our behavioural response to different situations is regulated by an underlying psychological structure known as our personality.

Fontana (1995) discusses the ways in which different notions of personality offer a variety of explanations of its impact on the child's emotional adjustment in the learning process. Some see human emotion arising from fluctuating constructions which are determined by the individuals' temperament, their past experiences and their circumstances.These are referred to as 'personality states'. A stronger form of personality approach would involve viewing the individual as having a predetermined 'personality type' or having particular 'personality traits'. In both of these the individual is seen as having relatively stable personality features which remain constant over time. A very soft form of the cookery book metaphor is evident in the notion of 'cognitive style'. Here relatively stable ways of interpreting stimuli are seen as forming a pattern of strengths and weaknesses in learning.

The early warning system

It's all in the genes. Emotions are perceived by selection theorists as inbuilt circuits that are used to respond to given situations. In its strongest form this metaphor sees emotion as the implementation of inbuilt survival reactions. We arrive in the world with all of our circuits wired up and they are activated by life experiences. What looks like learning in the child is nothing more than an organism searching through its library banks to find the appropriate response to given stimuli.

The sailing ship

An interactions perspective of emotions would see individuals as affected by and affecting their own affective stability. Just as the sailing ship is separate from the sea our emotions can be separate from the factors that have shaped them: hereditary, temperament, personality, and socialisation. The sailing ship is, however, strongly affected by the nature of the sea and the winds that influence it. The sailor can set his sail against the wind and tide and can make progress but that progress is likely to be painstaking. In the same way, individuals can cope with a variety of setbacks to their emotional development – loss, accident or injury, abuse, illness – and still emerge relatively intact.

The more effort and care that is put into constructing the sailing ship the more likely it is to survive storms. Thus effort put in to help children develop coping skills and a depth of insight and experience will enable them to cope better with difficult times. The underlying structure of an individual emotional resilience arises from:

- enjoying a wide range of experiences;
- coping well with fear and anxiety;
- building strong relationships;
- growing in a climate which sets clear boundaries and expectations;
- learning in an atmosphere where achievements are valued but everyone is safe to make mistakes without fear of damaging criticism;
- caring for physical health and well-being;
- receiving moral guidance and being taught to distinguish right from wrong.

Sometimes however the elements conspire to create circumstances in which even the best-appointed craft will founder. When the seas present insurmountable challenges the experienced sailor seeks a place of shelter to see out the storm. In the same way, sometimes the life experiences of the child are more than any child could cope with and at such times skilled help is often needed. For instance, children may need support to overcome illness or to cope with the loss of someone close to them.

Emotions, learning and school

By the time children arrive in school they have already reached a sophisticated stage of emotional development. Throughout their time in the primary school children continue to develop in complexity of response and in their insight into others' emotional state.

Smith, Cowie and Blades (1998) draw on a range of evidence to plot the following developmental path. From birth onwards children signal their emotion. Mothers can detect a variety of different emotions in their children in the first few months. From about seven months onwards fear responses, anger and pain show more strongly. Within the first year infants respond appropriately to the emotional expressions of their caregivers. Around the first year social referencing begins: children, faced with an unfamiliar situation, look to the caregiver to decide which reaction they should give; fear, alarm, anxiety and confidence can be transmitted in this way. From 18 month onwards a sense of self and an understanding of others develops. From two years onwards children can be seen using language to comment on and explain their own feelings. From three years of age children can deliberately manipulate emotions to achieve a certain effect on others. By four years children can take account of someone's desires in predicting their emotional state; they are not just basing their judgment on a stereotyped situation–emotion link. By six or seven years children learn to understand and manipulate emotions in a more complex way.

—Once emotions occur they become powerful motivators of future behaviours. They chart the course of moment-to-moment action as well as set the sails toward long term achievements. But our emotions can also get us into trouble. When fear becomes anxiety, desire gives way to greed, annoyance turns to anger, anger to hatred, friendship to envy, love to obsession, or pleasure to addiction, our emotions start working against us. Mental health is maintained by emotional hygiene, and mental problems, to a large extent, reflect a breakdown of emotional order. Emotions can have both useful and pathological consequences (LeDoux 1998).

Exercises to help explore emotions

1. Try a circle time type round.
   (a) All sit in a circle
   (b) Each person in turn completes the expression 'When I hear the word (???) I think of . . .'
       For (???) insert: Love, Joy, Surprise, Anger, Sadness, Fear
   (c) Go around the circle until each member of the team has completed one sentence for each of the above words.

2. Brainstorm as many different words as you can that are associated with emotions. Group them under different headings. Compare your results with the list at the end of this section.

3. Split into groups of three and use a force-field analysis to explore how the school can be made into a more emotionally secure environment for children and staff.
   In a force field you try to describe the current position in your school by describing all of those opposing features of the school which help create the current balance.
   (a) List those features which help to promote the pupils' emotional security under 'helping forces'.
   (b) Next list under 'hindering forces' the features of the school which are not helpful to the emotional security of the pupils. (This requires a degree of self-criticism and should be undertaken in an open and supportive context.)
   (c) Choose three helping forces you would like to build upon and three hindering forces you would like to diminish.
   (d) Draw your force field on a flip-chart paper. Present these in a plenary to draw up priorities and develop an Action Plan.

How Emotionally Secure is our School?

Helping Forces   **Hindering Forces**

List of words associated with emotions

The words were grouped in a cluster analysis (definition) by Shaver *et al.* (1987)

	Adoration			
	Affection			
	Fondness	Arousal		
	Liking	Desire		
Love	Attraction	Lust		Longing
	Caring	Passion		
	Tenderness	Infatuation		
	Compassion			
	Sentimentality			

	Amusement			
	Bliss			
	Cheerfulness			
	Gaiety			Relief
	Glee		Contentment	
	Jolliness		Pleasure	
	Joy	Enthusiasm		
	Delight	Zeal		
Joy	Enjoyment	Zest		Eagerness
	Gladness	Excitement		Hope
	Enthralment	Thrill		Optimism
	Happiness	Exhilaration	Pride	
	Jubilation		Triumph	
	Elation			Rapture
	Satisfaction			
	Ecstasy			
	Euphoria			

	Amazement
Surprise	Surprise
	Astonishment

		Rage		
		Outrage		
		Fury		
	Aggravation	Wrath		
	Irritation	Hostility	Disgust	
	Agitation	Ferocity	Revulsion	
	Annoyance	Bitterness	Contempt	
	Grouchiness	Hate		
Anger	Grumpiness	Loathing		Torment
	Frustration	Scorn	Envy	
	Exasperation	Spite	Jealousy	
		Vengefulness		
		Dislike		
		Resentment		

	Depression		
	Despair		
	Hopelessness	Dismay	Alienation

	Gloom	Disappointment	Isolation
	Displeasure	Neglect	
		Rejection	

Sadness   Agony
              Suffering
              Hurt
              Loneliness
              Anguish

	Glumness	Homesickness	Pity
	Unhappiness	Defeat	Sympathy
	Grief	Guilt	Dejection
	Sorrow	Shame	Regret Insecurity
			Embarrassment
			Insult

	Alarm	Anxiety
	Shock	Nervousness
	Fear	Tenseness
	Fright	Uneasiness
Fear	Horror	Apprehension
	Terror	Worry
	Panic	Distress
	Hysteria	Dread
	Mortification	

Key points

1. Emotions are essential for successful learning.
2. From a very young age children show that they experience a range of key emotions.
3. Emotion acts as a driving force, motivating towards specific goals.
4. Emotions have been explained through many theories, each contributing to our understanding while no one theory has the complete answer.

3 Principles

As we all know from experience, when it comes to shaping our decisions and our actions, feeling counts every bit as much – and often more – than thought. We have gone too far in emphasising the value and import of the purely rational – of what IQ measures – in human life. Intelligence can come to nothing when emotions hold sway (Goleman 1996).

There are many skills and principles that we need to hold in mind when working with children's emotions. The more understanding we have about how emotions work then the better able we will be to produce strategies that will help support our pupils' development. A good analogy here would be a ladder. The higher up we are the more we can take in the 'big picture'. We can understand the processes that children are experiencing when they are bereaved, for example. As we come down the ladder we develop specific techniques and strategies that we will apply to and support the pupil.

Core principles for working with children's emotions

Some of the following principles will be new, but many we have known intuitively for a long time.

- Learning is an emotional experience which involves confidence and risk taking.
- Emotional well-being helps or hinders learning, it is never neutral.
- Emotional development is not a linear process.
- Schools use learning processes to support positive emotional development.
- Through addressing the emotional needs of *all* children the most vulnerable will also be supported.
- The emotional climate of the staffroom is very important and the emotional climate of a school is a management issue.
- Children can become vulnerable to difficulties in emotional development for a variety of developmental and environmental reasons.
- Emotional difficulties can become a significant barrier to learning.
- Emotional difficulties are multi-faceted and therefore solutions are usually multi-faceted and pragmatic.
- Children can be taught to cope better in difficult times.

Interventions should follow the Law of Parsimony: small responses to small problems, more complex responses to complex problems. The emphasis should be on 'best fit' solutions and it is not necessary to know all of the background to a problem before starting to work towards a solution.

However, there are some key questions that need to be addressed:

- How would you describe the child's relationship with adults?
- What are some of the child's key emotions?
- What is the behaviour that concerns you achieving for them?
- Are there stressful past experiences in the child's life?

These points are examined more fully below.

The relationship

We need to look first at the relationship that children have with staff in schools and the principles and skills that can help us develop good relationships. The way in which individual children respond to you can provide a lot of information about how they are used to relating with adults. We can place common styles along a continuum.

1. **Secure attachment.** We are well aware of the children who seem comfortable and confident with us. They quickly settle and are able to express themselves and enjoy the one-to-one attention in a natural manner. They are able to separate from people they are attached to with little or no difficulty.
2. **Over attachment.** There are some children who seem to become quickly over familiar with the adult: young children wanting to sit on the adult's lap, for example. They seem to bond very quickly and would almost come home with you if you allowed them to. Leaving these children can be difficult and these children can quickly switch to negative feelings towards the adult or become excessively clingy. Friendships can follow a similar pattern. All or nothing type relationships, they seem strong but are really brittle. These children seem to crave excessive adult time. This can result in attention-seeking behaviour in class.
3. **Anxious attachment.** This type of response is not untypical of children who have experienced numerous foster care experiences. They wish to form a relationship with the adult but are fearful of being hurt. They have experienced close relationships many times with 'trusting' adults – only to be hurt. These children are quite likely to 'test' adults to see if they can be trusted. (How many children who become excluded from our schools could fit this category!)
4. **Indifferent attachment.** Children in this group give off an aura of independence. They do not need a relationship. They seem to have developed a distancing to protect themselves from the risk of being hurt through not becoming involved. They manage their emotions through avoiding them. They will often hurt other children and show little ability to empathise with the hurt they have caused.

Through reflecting on a relationship we can detect indications of previous attachment experiences. With such understanding we can modify our responses to be more caring and supportive of the child. When we fail to do so we are reacting negatively to the child's needs and often perpetuating the same pattern of responses.

Empathy

A key way to understanding the emotional world of children is through empathy. Imagine you are that child, imagine standing as they do. How do you feel inside? Are they happy and confident or are they angry, frightened or lonely? Empathy can be the bridge across to a child's inner world (see empathic solution on p. 46).

Responses

When talking with children note how they respond to your questions as well as their responses to different situations. Situations can be seen as posing challenges to children. How they respond will again indicate how they are feeling inside. For example, if they repeatedly get themselves kept in from play times, could they be telling you that they are afraid of being with their peers? If a child never brings the right materials for a piece of work, are they telling you that they are frightened of failing, of being shown up? Their responses can be seen as coping mechanisms to the challenges they face. It is worth remembering that children usually are trying to solve a problem, not be one.

In the examples below you can see that we can view a child's behaviour as an answer to a specific situational question. It is not difficult to work out the most plausible question that would give rise to such behaviour.

SITUATIONAL QUESTION		CHILD'S BEHAVIOUR
Can you play with peers?		Anxious and scared of being with peers, tries to
	ANSWER = NO	avoid them
Can you follow adult requests?		Argumentative and defiant
	ANSWER = NO	
Can you share with others?		Takes toys off peers and
	ANSWER = NO	refuses to share

Remember, behaviour is functional in that it achieves something for the child. For children with emotional difficulties it is often used to avoid something. Before you sit down with children read their records; how they have responded to past situations may give you the answers to many questions.

Children will usually not be able to explain why they are unhappy or angry. They will often not have the words to tell you. You will often need to act or ask questions on their behalf. Could it be that they are: embarrassed; disgusted; scared about what may happen; frightened of getting others into trouble? Or that they: feel it is their fault; find it too painful to tell you; believe all children experience the same; feel weak or a failure; don't like you; don't believe you can help; lack trust in adults?

Past experiences

The reasons for all behaviour are complex. We don't always know the reasons for our own behaviour. When we obtain information about a child's past experiences some light will often be shed. We do not need to analyse deeply a child's past to appreciate that children who have experienced traumas of some kind in their lives often, but not always, respond with some form of problem behaviour. Their traumas include not only family conflicts, bereavements, emotional/sexual/physical abuse, but also the trauma of illnesses. Usually the difficulties involve losses, rejection, poor role models, or identity and attachment difficulties. Through looking for explanations we are avoiding what is known as the 'fundamental attribution error'. This is the tendency to explain other people's behaviour in terms of enduring personal qualities, but to explain our own on account of the complexities of the situation. For example, if I am short tempered I will see it as a result of the pressures I am working under; if you are short tempered I tend to see it as an indication of what you are like. I can't see the situational factors that affect you, I can only see my own. It is your behaviour that influences me most. When I see me I see me and the situation, and I hope you do too. But when I see you, I just see you.

As a result of this process many children are labelled naughty or deviant when the truth that is they are responding to the pressures of the situations they find themselves in. A further factor is that if the child's behaviour affects me in some way, then I am even more likely to see it as the result of an internal intention.

We need to undertake a 'journalistic' type investigation. This will usually throw up clear indicators as to why a child is facing difficulties. Any unexpected change in behaviour can indicate that the child is under some form of stress. Any behaviour can be explained through many causes: what seems to be naughty, cheeky behaviour may in fact be displaced frustration caused through bullying.

Coping with a crisis

There are occasions when children face extremely traumatic events, thus all school staff need a basic understanding of crisis management. Tragedies have happened in schools, resulting in a need for us all to look at how we can make schools safer places.

When children are extremely distressed it may not be possible to talk and reason with them, they may so distraught that they are not able to think clearly. How can we help?

What is a crisis?

Coping with the demands that life presents is not a single passing act, it is part of an ongoing process. We do not see the difficulties we face each day because we have learned to cope with them so well. We each have a range of skills which enables us to manage a range of situations. We cope through our successful interaction with our world. But there are times, and this can apply to children as much as adults, when situations call for skills which we just do not have. For example, a child can be overwhelmed through feelings of loss for a loved one. They are unable to cope with the emotional turmoil that is taking place inside. (At such times we speak of 'falling apart', of 'going to pieces'. We do this to come back together in a new way to cope with a new world.)

A crisis reaction is not an abnormal reaction, it is best seen as a normal response to abnormal circumstances. These circumstances are threatening or hazardous and cause us to lose our emotional equilibrium. Either the individual develops new coping skills over a period of time or a more severe psychiatric breakdown may occur.

At such times when everything fails, we turn to others for help.

Types of crisis

A useful classification of crises, with appropriate supportive tasks, was put forward by Baldwin (1978).

1. **Dispositional crisis** is when an individual does not have the necessary information to solve a problem which is causing great distress. The supportive task is to focus less on the emotional upset but provide the appropriate information and solutions. For example an overweight child could be taught new eating habits.

2. **Situational crisis** is when unexpected external events occur such as the sudden loss of a parent. The emotional reactions can overwhelm the individual. The supportive task is to provide emotional support, routine and information. See also Chapter 9, Loss and Separation.
3. **Maturational crisis** can occur when children become overwhelmed by the tasks that they face at a certain period of normal growth. Common examples are the adolescent identity crisis, and the mid-life crisis. The supportive task is to offer emotional support, a focused plan for immediate actions and general information at an appropriate level of understanding.

Each of these will be affected by children's level of understanding the maturational stage they are at and their existing skills.

Principles and techniques for dealing with crisis

The more support we receive during and after a crisis the better we cope with it and the less emotionally distraught we feel afterwards. The nature of a crisis is that it is unexpected and unprepared for, therefore we rarely respond as we would like to. As a result we experience such feelings as guilt and anger, combined with sadness and helplessness. Having someone to talk things through with is essential. This enables us to express our feelings as well as reflect on the skills resources needed to manage the situation.

There are some key techniques for helping children in a crisis situation:

1. Always offer continuous support.
2. When talking with a child go for 'fine' detail: 'where did it happen? what were you wearing? This can help the child focus on small manageable aspects of the traumatic situation.
3. Work on those aspects that are of major concern to the pupil.
4. Always break down any tasks for the child to do into small manageable goals. Aim to move from the less severe aspect of a problem to the more severe.
5. Make sure there are benefits to the pupil with minimum effort and that they are within the pupil's ability.

When working in crisis situations remember that your emotional reaction will be communicated to others, whether you feel in control of the situation or not. The Emergency Services take immediate and strong control when they arrive at the scene of an accident, they do not ask if people will do certain tasks, rather they instruct them very clearly to do them. This gives off clear messages that this situation is not abnormal, it can be managed and that is what is being done. Be prepared likewise to give short, clear messages when a child is emotionally distraught.

Assess the danger level to the pupil. If you feel the child is in physical or emotional danger you will need to involve external support agencies. If it is appropriate, help the child to gain the necessary skills – for example, dealing with bullies. Always make and maintain contact with the child's legal guardians. If the child has physical symptoms refer to a G.P. Be sure to seek specialist support and advice if you suspect physical/sexual abuse, or if suicidal tendencies are shown.

Key points

1. How children relate to us tells us much about their inner world.
2. A method to understanding children is empathy.
3. We must be careful of the attribution error: children are more than their behaviour.
4. A crisis is a normal reaction to an abnormal situation.

---

4 Emotions in the Classroom

Children differ in how they respond to negative emotions. For example, some will act out aggressively when angry, while others will turn inwards and become depressed and passive.

Emotions and learning

As we have already seen, emotions motivate us to learn new information. They help us to organise information and guide our thoughts and actions. We can make sure our classroom is an emotionally supportive learning environment through utilising three key emotions.

1. **Interest** (curiosity) motivates exploration and problem solving. It helps children to feel alert and focused. Interested children have a strong desire to explore and find out more about the target of their fascination. When children are interested they remember more, understand more and attend better.
2. **Happiness** (joy) increases learning and development. When children are happy they are more confident and have more energy and self-esteem to learn effectively. This is why children learn so much through play, because it takes place in a positive emotional climate. We all share our thoughts and feelings more readily when we are happy.
3. **Security** (safety) is fundamental for children to learn new information. If they do not feel safe then it is in their best interests to protect themselves by shutting out new and potentially harmful information. Threats will lead to children's defence mechanisms being brought into action. Learning now becomes a low priority, survival is the issue. Reactions such as 'fight or flight' are triggered.

Developing positive emotions in the classroom

There are many factors which will influence how interesting a lesson is and how happy and safe children feel. These will include age, experiences, learning potential, individual differences, differentiation, and so on. However the following are key features for positive classrooms.

- Lessons contain change and movement.
- Relationships are built on trust and regard.
- Learning involves feedback and mastery.
- Behaviour has boundaries and agreed consequences.

You can run a check on your classroom by completing the questionnaire in Figure 4.1

How do we know if a child is secure and happy?

All children have an emotional 'thumb print'; this is how they uniquely display their feelings. Through getting to know children individually we can tell whether they are secure or not. The key is to look and answer the following.

1. Is there a balance between positive and negative emotions?
2. What is the child's most frequent emotional expression?
3. How intensely does a child respond emotionally?
4. How long does an emotion stay with a child?
5. Does the child show pure emotional expressions or a mixture?
6. How quickly does a child respond to emotional events?

There are no right or wrong answers to these questions, each child is different. We need to be sensitive to how children tell us they are feeling.

Relationships in the classroom

This is a topic central to how effectively children learn. Children are often motivated to please adults. If relationships were not that important, children could be permanently connected to computers. Computers can help, but for children, learning is something that takes place between people. The quality of the relationship is very important for effective learning to take place.

There are a number of key components which help create a positive relationship between child and adult. These include:

1. **Respect** This involves teachers and adults encouraging children to take responsibility for their learning to become 'agents of their own destiny'.
2. **Positive regard** This is achieved through increased interactions and knowledge of one another's strengths and challenges. It enables children to be valued for their uniqueness and complexity.
3. **Commitment** Short term difficulties are resolved through a determination to achieve mutually agreed goals.
4. **Mutual support** Because a child is often placed in situations where failure is possible the dynamic experience of learning and growing together is vital. The teacher will enable the pupil both to *feel* significant and to *be* significant.

Effective use of feedback

Since children cannot learn without making mistakes, the role of feedback cannot be underestimated. How a teacher gives feedback is very important as this is so often the main time when children relate with the teacher – over their mistakes and not their successes. The nature of negative feedback is that it can become emotionally charged and lead the child to feel at best angry and at worst disheartened and saddened. We need to give children good feedback. This means giving them information which they can use to influence future behaviour. Evidence shows that positive feedback, even when it is given in a neutral tone of voice, is more effective than negative feedback. Good feedback encourages new skills, independence and self determination.

**CREATING
AN EMOTIONALLY SUPPORTIVE
LEARNING ENVIRONMENT
M. O. T.**

This questionnaire is designed to help you assess those aspects of the classroom that can affect the emotional climate. It can enable you to highlight those areas that are going well and maybe some where you would like to make changes. There are no right or wrong answers. It can help you do a quick profile of your class.

**If you feel the answer to a question is YES then tick the box,
otherwise leave the box blank.**

THE CLASSROOM   **1**

1 Are pupils allowed to sit with their friends? ☐

2 Are there quiet areas for children? ☐

3 Do you feel trained to support students with low self-esteem? ☐

4 Are your displays colourful, creative and changed often? ☐

5 Does your classroom look like a good place to work? ☐

REWARDS   **2**

1 Are the rules in your class positive? ☐

2 Are you consistent and fair in the way appropriate behaviour is rewarded? ☐

3 Do you have a wide range of rewards? ☐

4 Do you feel your rewards are effective? ☐

5 Are children's efforts valued as much as their achievements? ☐

RELATIONSHIPS   **3**

1 Are you able to get to know children individually? ☐

2 Do you know children's qualities as well as their skills? ☐

3 Do children discuss out of school interests and activities? ☐

4 Are pupils given positive feedback on their work? ☐

5 Are all children given responsibilities in the classroom? ☐

COMMUNICATION   **4**

1 Do you feel you have the time to listen to children? ☐

2 Do you let children 'teach' you who they are? ☐

3 Are the views of pupils sought on key issues, eg bullying? ☐

4 Do you agree that 'all children have the right to be heard'? ☐

5 Are pupils involved in deciding class rules? ☐

Figure 4.1 Positive classroom questionnaire

FEEDBACK   5

1 Do you set targets through negotiation with the pupil? ☐

2 Do pupils assess themselves before and after learning? ☐

3 Are efforts linked to results? ☐

4 Are pupils taught to manage their time when working? ☐

5 Are pupils confident in making mistakes to learn effectively? ☐

LEARNING   6

1 Do pupils reflect on what happened and why as they progress? ☐

2 Do pupils use past learning experiences to plan new ones? ☐

3 Is time taken for pupils to make connections between information? ☐

4 Do pupils apply existing skills and knowledge to new situations? ☐

5 Do you use different groupings for different work? ☐

CONFIDENCE   7

1 Is effort valued as much as achievement? ☐

2 Are pupils' opinions valued? ☐

3 Do pupils know that 'broken feelings are cared for as much as broken bones'? ☐

4 Are pupils aware of their skills in different situations? ☐

5 Do pupils set and achieve realistic targets? ☐

STAFF SUPPORT   8

1 Do you feel able to ask colleagues for support? ☐

2 Are there clear procedures for obtaining formal advice? ☐

3 Are your school Support Services efficient and effective? ☐

4 Do you have opportunities for professional development? ☐

5 Do you feel part of a team? ☐

You may wish to construct a profile of your classroom. To do this count up your YES scores from each section. Then shade in the number of YESes in the appropriately numbered column – starting at the bottom.

AN EMOTIONALLY SUPPORTIVE LEARNING ENVIRONMENT
M. O. T.

Y
E
S

1   2   3   4   5   6   7   8

A positive environment

Positive classrooms have clear and realistic expectations which are expressed in positive terms. Children are involved in formulating, deciding and modifying rules. Appropriate behaviour is recognised and encouraged. All children have opportunities to succeed in learning and to experience positive relationships. The positive classroom focuses on children's strengths, so there are plenty of rewards and lots of encouragement.

Building relationships involves:

- Smiles: Personal smiles of recognition and acceptance (I see you and I value you).
- Proximity: Children need an emotionally secure base from which to explore.
- Touch: Most, though not all, primary children enjoy a hug. For older children a light touch is sufficient. Be sensitive to what touch may mean to different children. And remember to touch for their benefit.
- Words: Words are important at all ages. Make sure your intonation supports what you say and that your body language does also.
- Feelings: Treat feelings as important. Broken feelings are just as important as broken bones.

Emotions as barriers to learning

We often speak of learning as taking confidence and can recognise some children who are so frightened of failing that they make little effort to succeed. To understand this we need to recognise that learning is functional. We learn when our sense of who we are will be either maintained or enhanced. If we will be better able to deal with our world then we will be motivated to learn. Learning involves risk. To learn we have to open ourselves up and develop new boundaries of our knowledge. If we do not feel safe we will resist learning.

When children cannot risk learning they fall back on defence mechanisms to protect themselves and resist change. These defences distort the world so that negative emotions are avoided. They make the world one we would like to live in, not the world we do live in. For example, children who are angry at their parents for separating may **displace** their anger on to safe others in school; children with low self-esteem will use **escapism** to avoid difficult learning situations; and children who have negative feelings towards themselves may use **projection** and behave like a bully towards weak others.

If we look at the behaviour a child engages in we can often gain insight into what they are trying to avoid and what it is they really need. Their behaviour provides us with information.

The hidden chemistry

There can be a further barrier to a good relationship-developing. This happens when there is an instant antipathy between two people that is irrational and negative. With maturity, most of us know that such intuitive feelings are often wrong. But for children these can be barriers to their learning if they prevent a good relationship developing with school staff. A plausible explanation for why this happens is as follows.

The conscious mind looks for differences; it notices and focuses more on change and movement; it enables us to remember the facial differences between people and events. The unconscious mind is triggered by patterns of similarities. It is emotional, irrational and spontaneous. As I approach a child for the first time, memories can be triggered from their unconscious because I look similar in some way to a person they have known in the past. The unconscious memory that is stirred sends an emotional message to their conscious mind about me. If I am associated with a warm, caring uncle then the emotional memory is positive and the child will feel good about me. But if I provoke negative and hostile memories through association with someone the child did not trust then there is an emotional barrier between us. The barrier need not be permanent or irreversible but recognition and awareness is the first step towards addressing the problem. If we feel such a negative barrier exists then we should proceed with caution. It is not difficult to work with people you spontaneously get on with. The professional challenge is to build and improve those relationships where insight, understanding, effort and skills are needed. That is what makes us professional.

Physically we can be sensitive to the child's personal space, we can avoid touching early in the relationship. Our voice will need to be soft in tone. When we are close we can try to work on the same level as them rather than towering over them.

Emotionally we can seek positive emotional links, interests that we have in common with them, shared holiday destinations or taste in music. We can give a clear message by actively spending time to explore personal similarities and differences. It is wise to let the child determine the pace of the relationship. We can give children control through not making assumptions about their needs (Would you like me to help you with that?).

The emotional quality of the relationship is equally important for secondary aged pupils.

Emotional needs analysis

There are many childhood difficulties that we know cause emotional trauma. While there is considerable overlap for most traumas, it can be helpful to appreciate children's fundamental needs and how best to support them. Here are some examples.

UNDERLYING CAUSE	CHILD NEEDS	SUPPORT
Family conflicts	Information and understanding	Available adult and routine
Bullying	Safety and coping skills	Active adult support
Communication difficulties	Understanding, security and an adult	Strategies to facilitate communication and reduce anxiety
Bereavement and loss	Emotional support to express their feelings	An informed adult to give child permission and time to grieve

Our key aim is to understand the emotional distress children are experiencing. This will enable us to support them in ways which allow their experiences to become a part of their development, and to prevent negative emotional experiences being a permanent barrier to learning.

Changes in behaviour

Any change in children's behaviour could well be the result of some form of stress in their life. As with adults, children's behaviour changes under stress. We all tend to regress under stress. It sounds simple, but it is true. When we are faced with circumstances and events which emotionally overwhelm us we try to return to ways of comforting ourselves that worked in childhood. This is why eating is a common reaction to stress, likewise pulling or fiddling with hair and biting nails. If these behaviours gave us comfort when we were young then we are likely to carry out some similar form of behaviour when we are older. All children will react to stressful experiences, but we need to assess whether a child is reacting differently from the way most children of a similar age would react.

When working with distressed children always encourage them to express their feelings, give them understandable information, suggest coping strategies and stay with them.

Some children have lost trust in adults and will resist efforts by others to get close to them. Do not be surprised or put off by their efforts to reject you. If your support is the right thing to do, keep doing it. We shouldn't always worry about outcomes. The benefit of what you are doing may not be appreciated for a long time. Sometimes we may only 'catch' children as they 'fall', perhaps a colleague will move them on next year. This does not lessen the value of our role at all. It is still important.

When is a child vulnerable?

Children differ in their responses to difficult situations. Within the same family there may well be one child who seems to be coping well with difficulties at home. Another child – often a boy – may be showing a wide range of emotional and behavioural difficulties in school. Sometime adverse circumstances seem to 'steel' some children; it is as if they are determined to carry on as normal. How can this be explained? While the natural tendency is to focus on the child for explanations, we need to look both at the child and the child's environment. The better we understand both the more informed and successful our interventions will be.

However, before proceeding, we should consider why boys often react worse to difficulties than girls. A key factor is that boys are more vulnerable to negative emotions. This is a result of both their biology and social expectations. Boys are often encouraged to suppress their feelings or express them in aggressive, physical forms. When they do this in response to distress they find themselves experiencing negative and hostile reactions from adults instead of sympathy and understanding, which other more passive responses would obtain.

Temperament and defence mechanisms

Children are not passive recipients of all that happens to them: they actively shape and influence their environment. How they think about situations will naturally influence how they feel about them. Self-critical children will have difficulties in coping with unexpected test failure, but may cope with a family loss. As we have seen, they will be using a wide range of defence mechanisms, and this again will influence their responses. How children respond is their 'coping style'. There are two recognisable factors which influence a child's coping style; temperament and defence mechanisms.

Temperament

Thomas and Chess (1984) produced a tripartite classification for children's temperaments.

1. Easy temperament children tend to be adaptable and have a positive outlook. They are curious and persist in their explorations.
2. Difficult temperament children are far less flexible and become easily alarmed in new situations. They are prone to a negative outlook and have irregular and intense reactions.
3. Slow-to-warm up children, as the name suggests, take time to adapt, are reluctant to explore new situations and have a low intensity reaction.

It is clear that difficult and slow-to-warm-up children are more likely to be emotionally effected by stressful experiences.

Defence mechanisms

We have already mentioned some defence mechanisms that are used to reduce stress and protect a child's self-esteem. In addition to displacement (shouting at you feels good), escapism (another time, not now) and projection (I see my faults in you), children may resort to denial (what problem?), rationalisation (give the right tools), or regression (I'm too young to face this).

The environment

It is wrong to explain actions only in terms of themselves: the context in which they are facing difficulties is another equally important part of the equation. Schools and families have many expectations, rules and demands that are placed on children. Some of these will be pressures on children which may or may not be reasonable. Excessive control may result in some children becoming increasingly aggressive. For others it may lead to passivity. Because children have less power to change or control their environment than adults they are more prone to negative emotional reactions as a result.

When trying to decide what is appropriate support for vulnerable children, we need to ask ourselves whether they are responding in the way we would expect their peers to respond in a similar situation. If so, then it is more likely to be the environment that is the main cause, and we should seek to support them sensitively.

If on the other hand they seem to be over-reacting, or reacting adversely, when compared with their peers then we can look at ways of helping them develop better ways of coping and age appropriate skills. They are probably more vulnerable because of their temperament and/or the defence mechanisms they are using. Vulnerability is the result of an interaction between children and their environment.

The role of the school

Schools have a central role to play in supporting all children through adverse and difficult events. Our task in school is to make a difference where we *can* make a difference. It is not always possible or appropriate for a class teacher to work with children's families. We do not have the power to change their home circumstances but we can ensure that the school environment is emotionally supportive for all children, and especially those who are most vulnerable.

Research into what makes for an effective school has been undertaken for some time –

Fifteen Thousand Hours (Rutter *et al.* 1979) was the first to increase our understanding. We know that positive school environments can mitigate the effects of home stress, and recent research (Barber 1996) indicates that the characteristics of effective schools are as follows:

- strong positive leadership by head and senior staff;
- a good atmosphere or spirit, generated both by shared aims and values and a stimulating and attractive physical environment;
- high consistent expectations of pupils; high academic standards;
- a clear and continuous focus on teaching and learning;
- well developed procedures for assessing how pupils are progressing;
- responsibility for learning shared by the pupils themselves;
- participation by pupils in the life of the school;
- rewards and incentives to encourage pupils to succeed;
- parental involvement in children's education and in supporting the aims of the school;
- extra-curricular activities which broaden pupils' interests and experiences, expand their opportunities to succeed and help to build good relationships.

There are many ways in which schools can seek to support their children's emotional health. These range from developing coping strategies such as social and problem solving skills, to setting up peer support and contact with a chosen adult.

Support will be most effective when the aim is to enhance or restore normal skills which children of certain ages possess. The more such support is a natural part of the social context then the more likely is learning to take place. In everyday interactions children learn through the information they receive, observing other people and practising new skills.

These occur naturally as they play together and engage in shared activities. Any attempt to support children needs to take these factors into account. Because certain interventions work with adults it does not follow that they will automatically work equally well with children.

Note that children who have coped successfully with adverse circumstances usually have one significant, supportive adult. In times of stress and crisis children turn to teachers, support staff and friends.

Support groups

There are many ways of supporting vulnerable children and support groups are one such new development. There is now both research and information to enhance the effectiveness of such groups (Bennathan and Boxall 1996). To enhance their effectiveness a key aim of support groups must be to allow two way support. Support that is voluntarily offered rather than being constrained by obligations will be more effective.

Key points to consider when setting up a support group are: skills (What are the skills that the children will learn?); organisation (How will the group be set up? Are the leaders trained and who will monitor progress?); and learning (How will you ensure that learning has taken place?). Because learning is a core aim within any school this last question should be considered first.

Learning issues

For effective learning children need:

- to be involved;
- to know what it is that they are learning;

- to have opportunities to reflect on what they have learned;
- to generalise the information to new situations;
- opportunities to practise new skills.

Organisational issues

Before setting up a group each of the following needs to be considered:

- Recruitment
    Will the group have a special name?
    What are the core aims of the group?
    How many children will belong to the group? (5–10 is recommended)
    How many sessions will there be and what length?
    When and where will the sessions take place each week?
    How can disruption to other lessons be minimised?
    Will new members be allowed to join?
    Will the group be mixed or single gender?
    Is there a permanent place to meet?
    Will the children be of similar age and skills?

- Professional support
    Do you feel trained to run such sessions?
    Do you have colleagues to support you?
    How will parents be informed and consent obtained?
    Will parental consent be sought before or after the group has been selected?

Skill issues

A useful way to support children is to avoid the problem focused emphasis on what is or has gone wrong. Instead, focus on the solution: that is, what are the skills that children need to be happy and successful in school? The list below is the beginning of such a framework. Having identified areas that need improving or developing, support groups could be used for children to learn about the skills, see them, practise them and then try them out in real life situations.

- Classroom skills: listening, asking for help, saying thank you, asking questions, following instructions
- Friendship making skills: introducing yourself, beginning/ending conversations, joining in, asking a favour, giving a compliment
- Dealing with feelings: knowing your feelings, expressing your feelings, recognising others' feelings, dealing with anger, expressing affection
- Alternatives to aggression: using self control, responding to teasing, avoiding trouble, problem solving, negotiating
- Dealing with stress: dealing with boredom, making a complaint, dealing with losing, reacting to failure, dealing with embarrassment
- Feeling good: exercise, target setting, good news, positive statements, evocative words, humour, relaxation

Some examples of support group plans are given in Figures 4.2 and 4.3. Another well documented approach is that of circle time (Curry and Bromfield 1997).

SUPPORT GROUP PROGRAMMES

RECORD

SESSION..............

DATE.................

NUMBER OF PUPILS...............

LENGTH OF SESSION.....................

DESCRIPTION OF ACTIVITIES

PUPILS' RESPONSE

COMMENTS

TOPIC   *Using self-control.*
         Alternatives to aggression.

KEY DISCUSSION POINTS
What can children do when they feel
aggressive? How to stop kicking someone.
Observation. Trigger points, awareness
of situations.
Understanding of why they need
strategies.

ACTIVITIES
Stop Think Go!
Count to 10 – Time Out – a walk around
the playground, a time out space in school.
How did you feel before you wanted to
hurt someone – why?
Identify feelings, name and identify.
Self-esteem games – fun!
Putting on the brakes
Turn away – circle time game
question plus answer response
Playing games. role play, rehearsing
Listening skills game
Physical control games – musical statues.
Relaxation techniques.

RESOURCES
Book – 'he hit me back first'
Music
Tell it * Show it * Do it * Practise it

TOPIC   *Friendship making skills,*
         joining in.

KEY DISCUSSION POINTS
How to cope with rejection, how to
approach others, following the rules of a
game, appreciation of having been
allowed to play, pro-active involvement
of others.

ACTIVITIES/RESOURCES
Role plays.
'Who am I' party game.
Listing ways of being told
'you can't play' and discussing
them. Discussing sensible rules for any
game.

Tell it * Show it * Do it * Practise it

TOPIC   *Beginning and ending a*
         conversation.

KEY DISCUSSION POINTS
Very clear simple, specific
directions/instructions – SMART targets
Instigating conversations.
ACTIVITIES
Turn taking games – in a circle.
Asking questions/waiting. Listening to
and repeating answers.
Showing an interview, eye contact and
NVC
Politeness – hellos and goodbyes,
Please and Thank you.
Guessing games.
Modelling through role play.
Question and answer game, given the
answer, what's the question.

RESOURCES
BT Talkworks (Free phone booklet)
Friendship boxes.

Tell it * Show it * Do it * Practise it

Figure 4.2 Support group programmes

SUPPORT GROUP PROGRAMMES FOR CHILDREN OF CHEMICALLY DEPENDENT PARENTS

RECORD

SESSION ....

DATE   ....

NUMBER OF PUPILS ....

LENGTH OF SESSION ....

DESCRIPTION OF ACTIVITIES ....

....

....

....

PUPILS' RESPONSE

....

....

....

COMMENTS ....

....

....

....

TOPIC *Friendship making skills –
joining the group, making 'my
bag'*

KEY DISCUSSION POINTS
*Establish ground rules. Getting to know
each other through fun. Understanding
the aim of the group.*

ACTIVITIES/RESOURCES
Chart paper, crayons and white bags

METHODS
*Introduce group through games, explain
how everyone is here to understand and
learn how to cope with their family
difficulties and that chemical
dependency will be discussed as well as
ways for the children to have control
over their life. Children decorate their
bag and then put five things in the bag
that somehow describe who they are*

TELL IT * SHOW IT * DO IT *
PRACTISE IT

TOPIC *My feelings*

KEY DISCUSSION POINTS
Identifying and recognising feelings.

ACTIVITIES/RESOURCES
*Chart with different feelings, cards with
feeling words written on them, balloon,
post-its.*

METHODS
*Teach children about feelings and when
people feel different ones. Children
choose a feeling and explain, role play
it. Ballon used to explain what happens
when feelings are kept in. On post-its
children write how they are feeling and
stick it on chart.*

TELL IT * SHOW IT * DO IT *
PRACTISE IT

TOPIC *Chemical dependency is a
family illness*

KEY DISCUSSION POINTS
*Children learn that drug dependency
affects all the family and that they are
not to blame.*

ACTIVITIES/RESOURCES
Chart paper and crayons.

METHODS
*Discuss positive and negative effects of
drugs. How drugs affect people –
addiction. Challenge stereotypes and
stress how children can never make a
parent take drugs. Share ideas about how
children take care of themselves when
their parent is drinking or using drugs.*

TELL IT * SHOW IT * DO IT *
PRACTISE IT

Figure 4.2 Support group programmes for children of chemically dependent parents

Some guidelines for the use of humour in the classroom

Humour can be a very powerful tool. It can help to change a relatively dull topic into one of excitement and can therefore aid in the generation of strong episodic memories. There is a growing body of evidence to suggest that humour can be used to develop cognitive abilities. Certainly there is little doubt that a keenly developed wit is culturally regarded as an indicator of intelligence.

When used **positively** in the classroom, humour can enhance the creative process through: combating stress, improving self-esteem, enhancing social interaction, making life generally more interesting, and aiding the healing process. It can be an essential tool in the teacher's repertoire, as well as helping to make a good reputation. However, humour needs to be used with enormous care or it will be counter-productive.

Sadly, some of the most vulnerable members of our community may suffer from vicious humour. Some of the most cruel things heard in school are said in the name of humour. Often the cruelty arises from a lack of awareness of the impact of the comment on the individual who is hurt. When used negatively humour can be used to embarrass others, emphasise the social exclusion of others, create racial tensions, emphasise gender difference, increase exclusion of people with disabilities, be a component part of bullying, remind children of past difficult life circumstances.

Humour appears to be more important as children progress through the school as a predictor of peer acceptance and the children's self perception of their own social competence.

Fenwick (1996) discusses the use of humour in the healing process and suggests a number of strategies to help in reducing stress through humour and gives the following as ground-rules:

- Have an AT&T rule (i.e. all jokes must be appropriate, tasteful and tactful).
- Racist jokes are forbidden.
- Sexist jokes are forbidden.
- Laughing with people is compassionate, laughing at them is immoral and unethical.
- Appropriate humour never belittles or criticises.
- Humour should not stand apart from an ethos of caring and empathy.
- Humour should not be used to reduce the confidence of others in the group.
- Jokes should never be directed at weaker members of the group.

Sarcasm probably breaks all of the above rules and therefore should be avoided. Added to this should be humour which targets children/students who are differently able. We should challenge this just as we would any sexist or racist joke.

Using humour involves risk taking probably because it taps into all of our deepest emotions. For the sensitive but adventurous teacher the use of humour can make the difference between an adequate lesson and one that inspires and motivates.

Key points

1. Emotions are a natural part of learning, and can help and hinder.
2. Changes in behaviour often reflect emotional difficulties.
3. Children who have adult support cope much better with adversity.
4. Support groups can offer understanding, skills and fun.
5. Humour can inspire and motivate.

5 Self-esteem

We all appreciate the need for children to feel good about themselves and recognise that confidence is essential for children to 'risk' learning. Children who have a history of learning failure will approach new situations with an expectation to fail. The relationship between self-esteem and failure is two-way:

Failure can lead to a low self-esteem
and
a low self-esteem can lead to failure.

Good self-esteem has many benefits: we think more positively about ourselves and others; we are less prone to illnesses and enjoy new challenges; we usually have more friends and more fun.

Self-esteem is like oxygen. Children must have a good supply to thrive. Without it their behaviour can become frantic and dangerous if they 'act out' or passive and withdrawn if they 'act in'. Think of the children you have concerns about in your class and ask yourself, 'how good do these children feel about themselves?' Children with difficulties attract a smaller portion of the positives that other children get. They can become trapped in a vicious circle. Children can mask their low self-esteem with such behaviours as aggression, denial or projection. It is often sensible to treat our first concerns with children as symptoms that have reached the surface: the real problem lies beneath.

As children arrive for school we see their different shapes and sizes, the clothes they wear and the bags and boxes they carry. What we can't see are the pictures they carry of themselves inside their heads: how they think and feel about themselves. This will influence the kind of learner they are going to be. This is especially true for those children who are facing certain challenges. They may have sensory or physical challenges, one of many kinds of learning difficulties. Or they may face emotional and/or behavioural challenges. The last is often more difficult as it tends to attract negative responses from those around, not sympathy. This is understandable but within school we need to be able and prepared to work positively with all of our children.

Usually our understanding of any child, coupled with existing professional knowledge and expertise, will be enough for us to help children with low self-esteem. There will be times however when we are faced with children who do not respond to our usual methods and a more detailed and systematic approach may be necessary.

In this chapter we will both remind ourselves of the key principles related to self-esteem and consider a range of strategies.

Key concepts

While many of the key terms are frequently used, it is worth being clear as to their meaning here.

Self-concept
This is our overall view of who we are and encompasses a number of related aspects.

Self-image
This is how we see ourselves and comes from our realisation that we are separate from others. It is influenced by the feedback we receive from our carers. We see ourselves through the eyes of others. This is the 'looking glass theory of self'.

Ideal self
As we learn about who we are, we come to realise that there are certain standards of behaviour that are expected from us. We can be good or bad in the eyes of our carers. We learn that the adults who matter to us value certain traits such as honesty and cleverness, and because we wish to please them we strive to achieve their praise through possessing these traits. As a result we internalise an ideal self, how we would like to be. It is against this that we compare ourselves, we contrast 'how we see ourselves', with 'how we would like to be seen'.

Self-esteem
This refers to how much positive regard we feel towards ourselves. It is our evaluation of how far our self-image is from, or how close it is to, our ideal self. A healthy discrepancy can act as a motivator; problems arise when the discrepancy acts as a block – that is, we are so frightened of failing that we stop trying.

Children's self-esteem is clearly influenced by their experiences at both home and school. Most children have a good self-esteem which is supported from home. There will be some who experience times when their home life is not supporting their self-esteem. Thus what we do in school for all children is important, but for some children what we do is even more important.

In school, children need to have positive learning experiences and develop confidence and the motivation to learn. But, importantly, they need to feel accepted and valued. Young children especially have a very strong need to please the adults who care for them.

We understand much better today the factors that will affect a child's school success. Children's achievement is affected by their expectations; how they think about themselves, positively or negatively, begins early in their schooling. It is the first 10 years' experience which shapes their self-concept. Because primary aged children's self-esteem is incomplete and impressionable they are very sensitive to adult feedback. They are vulnerable to negative learning experiences and can develop a low self-expectation of being able to learn. How we talk about children will affect their self-esteem, so we must be very careful of the language we use to ensure that we are having a positive influence and not a negative one.

Building self-esteem through positive classroom management

To promote a positive self-esteem in children we need to ensure that they have a safe supportive learning climate. They need to know that they are valued unconditionally, that they will be listened to, and that they have unique interests and qualities. Because learning involves making mistakes, these mistakes are seen as opportunities for learning not for being put down. All pupils will be given lots of opportunities to learn manageable amounts of information or skills and given time to show what they have learnt or can do. This will be their output which will enable us to give feedback – hopefully, praise for their success.

If learning is seen as a competitive activity there will be those children who believe that they have no chance of winning or those who lack the confidence to risk losing. Such a climate will be the conditions for either withdrawal or disruptive behaviour as a way of avoiding even entering into such a competition.

Some guidelines for nurturing and developing self-esteem in the classroom are:

1. Always expect the best from children (This shows you have faith in them.)
2. Make learning objectives clear (This shows that your lessons are planned, purposeful and enables children to relate goals to existing knowledge as well as motivating them.)
3. Reward and praise them all often (This will enhance and strengthen their confidence.)
4. Value their efforts and achievements (This will show them that effort and determination to learn are valued qualities.)
5. Involve them in setting learning targets (This will promote independent learning.)
6. Make time to get to know their personal qualities and interests (This will show that you value them as unique people.)
7. Be hard on issues but caring towards people (This will show that you will not tolerate behaviours which prevent you from teaching and them from learning. But at all times they – the pupils– are okay.)

Positive teacher qualities and behaviours

One way of changing children's behaviour is to change your own. Positive teacher qualities and behaviours are a significant factor in promoting children's self-esteem in the classroom, in particular:

1. Understanding (Be aware of the needs and challenges children face.)
2. Encouragement (Give as much attention to effort as to achievement.)
3. Sensitivity (Appreciate children's heartfelt need for success and recognition.)
4. Expectations (Have fair but high expectations.)
5. Respect (Value children for their own qualities, skills and strengths.)
6. Challenge (Give diverse and interesting work and targets that are relevant to individual children.)
7. Creativity (Use pupils' imagination and existing knowledge to involve them in new experiences.)
8. Planning and organisation (Understanding of a subject is shown through schemes of work being in place. Checklists are used to monitor progress on agreed learning targets.)
9. Effective classroom management (Behaviour in class is always a management issue. Misbehaviour prevents learning and is dealt with positively but firmly.)
10. Sense of humour (Humour allows for shared enjoyment as well as opportunities to release tension.)

To achieve a caring and accepting classroom, teachers need constantly to step back and consider their own core behaviours. For instance, do you show a warm positive attitude towards pupils? Have you established democratically positive rules, and do you enforce the rules consistently and compassionately? When you talk to the children do you use open ended questions and does your manner encourage diversity in personalities, activities and responses? Are you teaching pupils to self-evaluate positively? Have you planned carefully to ensure that *all* pupils can experience success? And do you listen undividedly when needed? (See Figure 5.1).

**GUIDELINES
FOR DEVELOPING SELF-ESTEEM**
an aide mémoire

Take a long term perspective

Find the positive changes

Show faith

Build self respect

Recognise effort and improvement

Focus on strengths and assets

Build on existing strengths

Use small steps to ensure success

Make praise appropriate

Record successes

Look for novelty

Catch them being good

Help them find their skills

Have fun

Make trying safe

Figure 5.1 Core behaviours for teachers

Praise and encouragement

Praise is central to any teacher or support staff's repertoire, but how often do we stop to think if we are using it effectively? The reward of praise is most effective when it relates to a clear achievement and is given personally and generously to pupils as soon after their success as possible. Its effectiveness is increased by children knowing precisely what they are being praised for.

Encouragement differs from praise in that it is given for effort, improvement or interest. Encouragement shows appreciation of a child's assets. It gives value to the child's efforts. Encouragement is a gift that can be given freely, because everyone deserves it.

Self-esteem and relationships

There is today a better understanding of how learning takes place and which conditions support it. We know that the brain is social in nature and is always searching for patterns and meaning. We also know that learning is enhanced through emotions. This can be best understood if we consider negative emotions.

In schools, we need children to feel emotionally confident and safe so that learning can take place. We want strong positive emotions to ensure that they remember the information and skills they are faced with. Because children learn best from those they trust and care for we need to explore the types of relationships we have with children.

As we try to tease out the different kinds of relationships we must be careful to remember that these are descriptions of complicated processes. In reality we move in and out of several relationships in very short periods of time. A helpful model has been suggested by Deiro (1996) – see Figure 5.2.

Each interaction has an essential part to play in creating the most appropriate relationship between adult and child. When we have such relationships we can observe certain characteristics. Emotionally supportive relationships show genuineness and authenticity and promote internal self-control. They contain expressions of humour and fun and are based on a non-judgemental approach.

Building positive relationships

We communicate constantly with our children. Because they are taking in the messages we pass to them we need to be careful of what we say. How we talk to them will affect how they feel about themselves. Establishing good relationships can be a definite way to support positive communications between adults and children. By acknowledging what the function of our communications should be – to support a child's self-esteem, identity and learning – we can look at methods which will help us achieve this. These can be practical things that become part of our classroom practice and identity.

One-to-one time

Any time we can spend with a child will be invaluable. When we give them our undivided attention we reach to their core. We listen with our eyes, ears and heart at

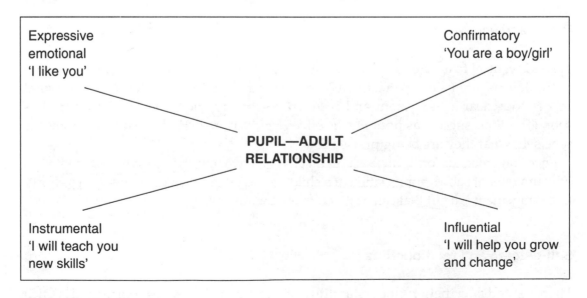

Figure 5.2 Types of classroom relationships

such times. One-to-one could be a special signal from me to you, a thumbs-up or a wink. Such moments are not trivial to their receivers.

Self-disclosure

Appropriate disclosure is a good method for moving beyond the roles that we each fulfil, pupil–teacher. Knowing what our favourite meals or TV programmes are helps to build a relationship which contains personal information.

Rituals and traditions

Within any class there can be certain practices which make sense only to those in the know. Like a private joke. Teachers can develop with their class unique ways for welcoming new children to their class, or special activities which can happen only when certain preconditions have been met.

Community identity

With such an increase in movement children do not always experience that sense of belonging that was so common in the past when people grew and married within the same community. Displays which reflect a class's movements/activities through the year can be helpful. Similarly class photographs enlarged around the room can reflect successes. A class photo at the end of each year can become a cherished memento for many children.

Parental involvement

Involving parents was easier when we all lived in the same community. Today we need to reach out so much more. We need to see parents as being equal partners and part of the solution. Ways that seem to have little success in involving parents need to be critically questioned. Parents want good and plentiful information about their children. Newsletters, telephone contact, home–school diaries and the like each have a role to play. In addition to PTA activities and school–home visits, parent groups to share concerns and ideas can also help.

Childhood stress

Children today face more stress than ever before. Evidence shows that there is an increase in many childhood disorders. There is more depression in children, more anorexia nervosa and bulimia. The causes are many and inter-related and include changing work patterns, secularisation of society, changing family patterns and the influence of the media. These changes are found in all modern countries and all report increases in childhood psychopathological conditions. There are however many everyday stresses that all children face. These can be coped with by most but for some they can become the enemy of self-confidence and lead to them experiencing worse difficulties. Those that believe childhood is a care-free time have perhaps forgotten the reality of the following: bullies, changing schools, conflict with teachers, competitive culture, toiletting, dental appointments, peer conflicts, parental difficulties, illness, violent TV, family unemployment, school failure, speaking in public, lack of parental interest, sibling rivalry, body shape, parental pressure to achieve, failure to complete homework, parental separation, bereavement, not being chosen for a team, anxiety about leaving home and going to school.

All of these can drain children's emotional reserves. The less confident they are then the worse they are going to be at dealing with any one of them. Such stresses will lead to the child becoming aroused and preparing for a flight or fight response. It is only children with a positive emotional reserve who will be able to manage the arousal and take more appropriate action (see Figure 5.3).

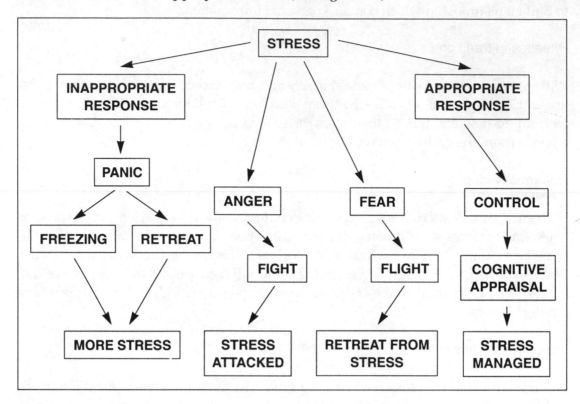

Figure 5.3 Responses to stress

Ideas and strategies for building self-esteem

There is no quick way to give children who lack self-esteem the confidence they need. Their self-esteem has been reduced over time, thus time will be needed to replace it. There are many ways of raising children's self-esteem. The skill is to select those best suited for that particular child. It is an art not a science. You will know the child in question best and this knowledge will guide you to the most appropriate strategies.

Self-esteem assessment

Look at what gives individual children their positive self-esteem. What is it that they get fun from? Who do they enjoy being with? What do they enjoy doing? Use the form in Figure 5.4 and try to write something under each of the areas.

Having identified what areas are giving the child positive input, make sure these are maintained and made as effective as possible. Choose an area that you have some control over. How could you make it better? Think of a goal you could work towards and use the plan in Figure 5.5 (p. 40).

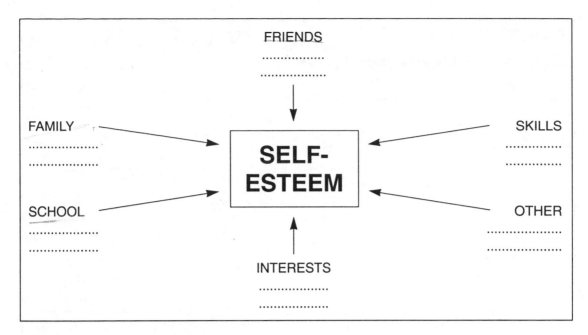

Figure 5.4 Assessing self-esteem

The act of helping

Strayhorn (1988) emphasises 'helping' as an activity that will help children with low self-esteem and give them a sense of well-being. There are two aspects to this activity: being helped and being the helper.

In a 'helping' activity, one person has a difficulty, another person offers to help and their offer is accepted. A way is then devised to solve the problem, the plan is implemented and the difficulty is overcome. The helper feels good for being of use, the person helped feels grateful for being assisted. There is an exchange of goodwill between the two.

In addition to setting up such activities for children who need to feel good, you may also allow them to observe acts of kindness in order to see the process at work. The positive aspects of such activities include awareness of feelings, recognition of needs, social conversation skills, empathy, trust and dependency, belonging, problem-solving skills, decision-making skills, care, cooperation and kindness. The act of helping can therefore be a very powerful activity!

Empathy as a core quality

It is possible for children to have a 'false self-esteem'. That is, they feel valued, know their own skills and set realistic goals; but they lack an essential quality, they lack care and respect for others. There are times when we meet other people who are low and not very happy with themselves. While we may feel good, we are able to detect their sadness and we tone ourselves down to more appropriately reflect their mood. This is through 'empathy'. We put ourselves into the shoes of other people and imagine the world from their view-point. This reflects both our care and respect for them.

Most children are able to put themselves in the shoes of their peers. They are able to: describe how another child feels in different situations throughout the day; explain how a child feels when they succeed or fail in school; give a range of feelings another child will feel when they are told off by adults.

GOAL SETTING

What would you like to achieve, be precise?

....

....

....

....

WHAT WILL:
   HELP   **HINDER**

....

....

....

....

WHAT COULD YOU DO TO ACHIEVE THE GOAL?

....

....

....

....

CHOOSE THOSE STRATEGIES THAT YOU FEEL ARE REALISTIC

....

....

....

....

The Appendix Section 1 contains further ideas and strategies.

Figure 5.5 Improving self-esteem

Children who lack empathy are unable to respect and care for others. Theirs is therefore a one-sided self-esteem, and not genuine. There are ways such children can be helped to 'put other children's shoes on' and describe how other people feel. You can tell them stories and ask them how key people are feeling. Enable them to help other children and then describe how they felt about helping and how they feel when they are helped.

Ask them to describe the feelings associated with different situations, such as loss of favourite toy, death of a pet. Give them the words to describe different feelings: ' I bet that made you angry/upset/sad/confused/lonely'.

Rewards and positive feedback guidelines

Children who have a low self-esteem will often refrain from certain behaviours that we know to be good for them. They may avoid joining in games with other children or avoid eye contact. Their behaviour is less often rewarded because they are trapped in a negativity cycle: they become used to negatives. Because they expect to be ignored or unsuccessful they behave in ways which result in this happening.

The way to break this negativity cycle is to give rewards whenever children do behave in a more positive way. Thus they are allowed the pleasure of receiving praise from an adult. If your rewards are not producing the desired effect on their behaviour then you may need to give more thought to how you are applying this strategy. For example, are you sure that what you are offering is rewarding? Have you asked the children what they like? Have you observed the children during free time to see what activities they enjoy taking part in? Do you know which events they seem happy after taking part in? Are you sure they will make some effort to obtain your reward? Often we make the assumption that what we like will be equally pleasing to others but a reward is appropriate only if a child will work to obtain it.

Presenting a reward after a particular behaviour will increase the likelihood of that behaviour happening again. By using rewards we can encourage children with a low self-esteem into behaviours which result in them receiving rewards, thus discouraging their tendency to take part only in behaviours which produce negative feedback. The principles are:

1. Make sure children are clear about the specific behaviours expected and the reward that they will receive.
2. Reward them immediately after the behaviour happens.
3. Be consistent in giving rewards.
4. Once the behaviour happens frequently begin to reinforce partially, for example after it occurs a fixed number of times, or after a set period of time has passed.
5. If children becomes less interested in the reward, reduce the size. If they seem unwilling to work for a reward you feel they would like to have, give it once or twice for free and consider increasing the size of the reward they can earn.
7. Vary rewards. Avoid the reward becoming too routine and mechanical; have a menu of rewards. For example, after a few 'well dones', switch to 'you really are working well today'.

Using these ideas you can involve children in earning more and more positive feedbacks. This will help boost their confidence and give them more confidence to try new behaviours. Their very body posture will change and their approach to new situations will reflect this increased confidence.

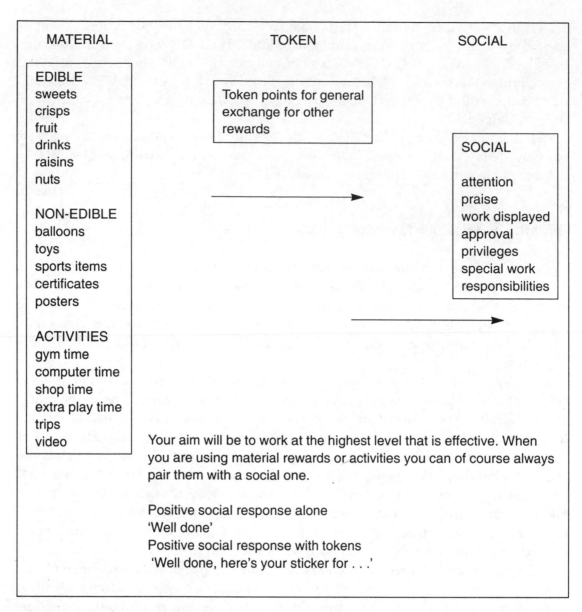

Figure 5.6 Types of reward

Some people may be unhappy about rewarding children, seeing the reward as a 'bribe'. It is worth remembering that a bribe is something you give to get someone to do something either immoral or illegal. It is not bribery to reward a child for doing something in their own interest.

Identifying rewards

We need now to consider different types of reward (see Figure 5.6) . The easiest and most effective rewards are adult attention, praise and approval. And what makes these especially good is that you always have these with you. However, there will be children who do not respond to these for many reasons. At such times we will need to use material rewards and activities. While we would prefer to give social rewards like praise, we can still work towards this.

Key points

1. Self-esteem is to learning what oxygen is to breathing – essential.
2. Positive classroom management will ensure confident pupils.
3. Personal awareness and understanding will ensure pupils are treated with care and respect.
4. How we communicate with our pupils tells them how we feel about them.
5. Pupils with low self-esteem can be supported through specific strategies.

6 | Understanding Motivation

Reluctant and resistant learners

In education, motivation is the term we use to explain why one pupil persists at a task, while another gives in at the first obstacle; why one pupil needs little direction and supervision while a peer needs constant reminders; why one pupil arrives with the correct equipment for a lesson while another rarely comes equipped; why one pupil volunteers for extra activities while another can hardly wait to get out of the classroom; why one pupil with less ability achieves higher grades than another of higher ability. The definition of the term motivation, for teachers, is the degree of effort, interest and involvement that a pupil has with a task.

The problem with motivation – or lack of it – as an explanation for the behaviour of reluctant and resistant learners is that it can too easily put all the responsibility for change on to the pupils. They are the problem, therefore the solution is within them – we cannot become motivated for them. Yet motivation is not a static, measurable thing that exists within a pupil's head. We need to consider factors that can help or hinder a pupil's motivation, including physical and medical factors, the pupil's learning ability, fear of failure and self-esteem. In addition, we all know how quality lessons engage us and how inspirational teachers fire us. Clearly, then, there are times when motivation is just as much affected by external factors – such as teaching style, lesson structure, feedback and consequences – as internal ones.

Key motivation questions

When trying to decide if a pupil is or is not motivated ask yourself these questions:

- Do you know the pupil, his or her values, hopes, needs and expectations?
- Are the learning outcomes challenging and obtainable through the learner's existing skills?
- Are there plenty of opportunities for success?
- Have you set meaningful targets and involved the pupil?
- Do you give regular feedback, reinforcement, recognition and praise?
- Are you sure the learner has the necessary resources?
- Does the learner understand the need and validity of the task?
- Does the pupil fail to make a reasonable or consistent effort to learn; rarely request help when they do not understand; fail to complete set assignments; need frequent reminders to pay attention; refrain from participation in class activities?

A positive approach

Unmotivated students can be intentionally resistant to involving themselves and may actively disengage from learning. When faced with unmotivated pupils teachers commonly become angry and hostile, or give up and withdraw support. As a result the pupil is perceived as the 'problem', the teachers have lower expectations and feel guilty over their lack of success. A more positive approach is to check all the factors involved:

Internal factors
Is the pupil able to manage the work?
Is the pupil aware of the learning targets?
Does the pupil enjoy learning new skills?
Does the pupil seem frightened of failing?
Is the pupil unmotivated in other areas of the curriculum?

External factors
Are there any changes at home?
Is the pupil being bullied?
Is the pupil well fed and cared for on arrival in school?
Has the pupil experience unexpected failures?
Are there good external motivators?

If none of these seem to apply then it can help if we reframe our view of the pupil and endeavour to see the world through his or her eyes. We need to explain the gains for the pupil in any learning situation, consider the quality of the materials and the teaching style, and make sure that the task is within the pupil's ability. We should accept some resistance as normal. If pupils have the energy to resist they have the energy to learn.

Theories of motivation

There are many theories of motivation (see Figure 6.1). Each has at its heart fundamental assumptions about human beings. Are they pushed from within into action, are they pulled along by outside forces, or do they have the ability to decide what to do? The first two are mechanistic in believing that the only way to explain human actions is through forces. The third believes that we have the ability through volition to initiate actions in our own right – that is, that we are the originator of what we do.

The answer is probably that each theory has an element of truth. But as we are looking to make sense of pupils' behaviour in the classroom we will focus on pragmatic approaches that offer us a commonsense understanding and enable us to support pupils who are failing to achieve their potential.

Gains of unmotivated behaviour

Before we begin to look at positive ways to motivate pupils we need to remember that there are gains to pupils' lack of motivation. Unmotivated pupils are understandably not achieving their full potential, they are in fact under-achievers. (Note that a different term to describe their behaviour can change attitudes towards them: they are now more victim than perpetrator.) However, persistent unmotivated behaviour is often maintained by a number of factors, such as extra attention – either through coaxing or hostility; kudos, real or imagined, from peers; avoidance of difficult work.

Theoretical-assumption that we are:	Example	Key proponent
biologically pushed	psycho-analytical	Freud
environmentally pulled	behaviourist	Skinner
pushed and pulled	gestalt	Lewin
needs led	need for achievement	McClelland
	hierarchy of needs	Maslow
thought led	attribution theory	Kelly and Hewstone

Figure 6.1 Theories of motivation

Motivating the unmotivated

We will now look at pragmatic approaches to improving matters. But first check that your answers to the following questions are yes.

- Are you sure that the pupil is not experiencing learning difficulties, requiring a more differentiated curriculum?
- Has the pupil the necessary learning skills for success? (Can they listen in class, organise themselves?)
- Are you sure that there are not any physical/medical reasons for the change in work? (Would a medical examination be worth considering?)
- Are you sure that there have not been any changes at home, such as family bereavement, stress? (If there are, discuss concerns with key people and, if appropriate, involve pupil in deciding how support can best be given.)

The empathic solution

This is an easy to use method for gaining insight into a pupil's needs and meeting them in appropriate ways.

Because emotions can act as barriers (see Chapter 4) we should try to establish what are the dominant emotions that any pupil is experiencing. If we ask the right questions we may be able to gain some insight into what the pupil is feeling. From this we can gain immediate ideas to address their emotional needs and increase their need or learning through mastery.

Empathic questions

What is the pupil's typical day? Describe it as they would experience it.
How do you think the pupil feels about your efforts to support them?
How does the pupil feel on arriving in school?
How does the pupil feel in your lesson?

What is the behaviour obtaining for the pupil?
Does the pupil behave inappropriately in front of other children? If so what is this behaviour achieving for the pupil?
Does the pupil behave inappropriately in front of adults? If so, what is this behaviour achieving for the pupil?

How does the pupil respond to adult direction?

Does the pupil hurt other children or spoil their work?

What are the pupil's key feelings?

Select the key ones from the list: anger, anxiety, confusion, fear, panic, loneliness, isolation, jealousy, inadequacy, sad, depressed, frightened, worried, scared, embarrassed, hurtful, flat, nervous, rejected, unloved, lonely, envious, aimless, lost, tearful.

Empathic solutions

What could you do to support this pupil and change his or her emotional expectations? A pupil Empathy Profile sheet is shown in Figure 6.2, overleaf.

Motivational mapping

With this approach we will analyse the key components of motivation and then decide more focused interventions to support pupils.

Many key motivational concepts have entered our educational language to explain some pupils' lack of motivation, for example 'fear of failure'. Rather than include them as discrete explanations we can link them together into a model of assessment known as 'motivational mapping'. The model proposed here (Figure 6.3) is one that enables an adult, either with a pupil or on their behalf, to explore what may be the causes of their under-achievement.

We shall consider seven main areas which can explain under-achievement in school. Once you have identified an area that seems to be acting as a barrier for the pupil you are working with, you will then be able to draw on strategies specific to that difficulty. Such diagnostic assessment allows more precision in our interventions, which not only saves time but makes our support more effective.

A map can also usefully help the pupil conceptualise what is going on, and in older children may promote active involvement and commitment. It is helpful to think of each area as an aspect of motivation, a spoke in the student's 'motivational wheel'. If one of the spokes is short then the student will experience a bumpy ride.

Strategies

From your assessment you will be able to identify the 'short spokes'; with the pupil select one or two areas to focus on. The seven spokes of motivation are presented below, each with five example interventions. Choose from these or add your own to improve the problem areas.

Awareness

1. Work with the pupil to develop:
   a) personal awareness
   b) recognition of skills
   c) personal value and responsibility
   d) problem-solving skills
2. Explore with the pupil the conditions that enable them to learn best. Try to incorporate these ideas into your support.
3. Pair the pupil with a motivated pupil to gain awareness and understanding of how they respond and the gains they receive.

PUPIL EMPATHY PROFILE

EMPATHIC QUESTIONS

Describe the pupil's typical day – as they would experience it.

How do you think the pupil feels towards your efforts to help them?

How does the pupil feel as they arrive in school?

How does the pupil feel in your lesson?

FUNCTIONAL ANALYSIS OF BEHAVIOUR

Does the pupil behave inappriately in front of other children? If so – what is the behaviour achieving for them?

Does the pupil behave inappropriately in front of adults? If so – what is the behaviour for them?

How does the pupil respond to adult direction?

Does the pupil hurt other children or spoil their work?

WHAT ARE THE PUPIL'S KEY FEELINGS?

EMPATHIC SOLUTIONS
What could you do to support this pupil?

Figure 6.2 Finding empathic solutions

TEST USER INSTRUCTIONS

1 Answer each of the questions quickly, *yes* or *no*

2 Then transfer your scores to the map (motivational wheel) below

3 If you have more appropriate questions for the pupil then insert one of yours instead of one of these.

4 If there are areas that score the same choose the area where you can expect improvement to be achieved.

STUDENT ASSESSMENT

NAME ....

DATE ....

ASSESSED BY ....

INDICATIVE QUESTIONS

These are Indicative Questions; you may have more appropriate ones that you may wish to ask.

1. AWARENESS

1. Is the pupil aware that they are under-achieving?   Y/N
2. Has the pupil made efforts to improve?   Y/N
3. Can the pupil explain how they feel about the difficulty?   Y/N
4. Is the pupil aware of the effect their behaviour has on others?   Y/N
5. Is the pupil aware of the consequences to their behaviour?   Y/N

2. REWARDS

1. Will the pupil work to obtain tangible rewards?   Y/N
2. Can the pupil explain how they feel when they help others?   Y/N
3. Does the pupil enjoy social praise?   Y/N
4. Can the pupil name three activities they enjoy?   Y/N
5. Can the pupil describe past positive feelings?   Y/N

3. CONFIDENCE

1. Can the pupil manage constructive feedback?   Y/N
2. Is the pupil relaxed in new learning situations?   Y/N
3. Is the pupil always in school for tests?   Y/N
4. Does the pupil readily try to answer questions?   Y/N
5. Do you feel confident about this pupil's approach to learning?   Y/N

4. CONTROL

1. Is the pupil able to set realistic targets?   Y/N
2. Does the pupil see success in terms of themselves?   Y/N
3. Is the pupil able to be a leader in some situations?   Y/N
4. Does the pupil enjoy classroom responsibilities?   Y/N
5. Does the pupil contribute in group discussions?   Y/N

Figure 6.3 Motivational mapping – the test

5. PATIENCE

1. Is the pupil able to defer immediate gratification?   Y/N
2. Can the pupil follow class rules to obtain teacher attention?   Y/N
3. Is the pupil able to cooperate and take turns in games?   Y/N
4. Can the pupil adjust their pace for slower peers?   Y/N
5. Is the pupil able to contain frustration and anger?   Y/N

6. RELATIONSHIPS

1. Does the pupil show self-confidence with peers?   Y/N
2. Is the pupil able to express different views to their peers?   Y/N
3. Is the pupil confident when away from their friends?   Y/N
4. Can the pupil assert themselves over their peers?   Y/N
5. Is the pupil more of an individual than a group member?   Y/N

7. ACHIEVEMENT

1. Does the pupil enjoy the success of learning?   Y/N
2. Is the pupil competitive in games and sport?   Y/N
3. Does the pupil enjoy having choice in what they learn?   Y/N
4. Do you believe the pupil expects to succeed?   Y/N
5. Does the pupil persevere with difficult tasks?   Y/N

MOTIVATIONAL MAPPING

Shade in your scores for each area in the motivational wheel.

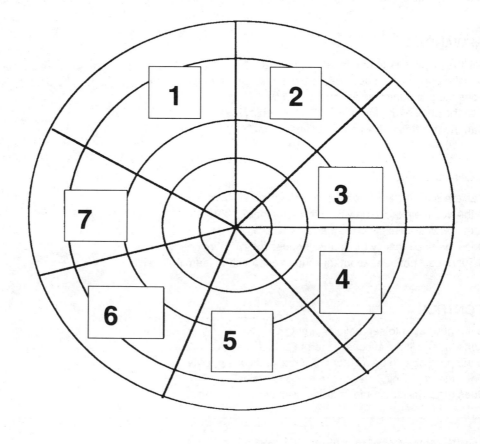

4. Explain that not being interested in every subject is permissible, but this does not justify not working. Make the consequences for not working clear.
5. Monitor and review work output over a set period.

Rewards

There are pupils who seem to have no skill deficiencies, only an apparent lack of motivation. We may observe that they will help others, seem to pay attention, will work to a set goal, but only when there are immediate positive consequences. Whereas most people experience a warm glow from performing acts of kindness, these pupils feel nothing, there is no internal pay-off. They lack the internal skill of rewarding themselves and show us the behaviour only when there is extrinsic reward.

There are two clear skills involved with motivation – the skill of performances and the skill of internal positive feedback. The latter skill – the ability to feel good inside when we do something we are pleased with – is referred to as **intrinsic motivation**. The following interventions are aimed at developing this skill of intrinsic motivation in those pupils who currently respond only to extrinsic rewards.

1. Pictures: Think of a memory that makes you feel really good. Try to get inside that 'feeling good'. If the feeling was an animal what kind would it be? If the feeling was a sound, what sound would it be? If the feeling was a colour what colour would it be? Now imagine a task you want to succeed in. Picture yourself doing the task. You are just completing it. What are the feelings you have for completing the task? If you are unsure, imagine your animal, or colour, or sound that makes you feel good. Keep practising.
2. Words: Choose two or three words from the following list that you like: strong, happy, powerful, love, peace, helpful, will-power, can-do, calm, sunny, purposeful, determined, kind, caring. Now practise using those words whenever something goes well. Write them down in your book. Try each day to use your words after you have been successful in completing a target you set for yourself.
3. Good deeds: Think of how you felt when someone, at home or in school, helped you. Remember how you felt inside to be helped in a way that was just right. Remember or imagine helping someone who really needs your help: picture the scene. Where are you? What are you wearing? Now let yourself feel some of those feelings that you know happen when people help each other. Each day make sure you use some of these activities.
4. Set a menu of positive consequences that could be achieved for certain learning targets being achieved. Make sure that any positive consequences are worked for. Try to set up a 'positive entrapment programme' whereby the pupil cannot help but achieve success and receive rewards for their attainments and/or efforts.
5. Develop a positive image of learning. Pair learning success with 'street cred' rewards – CDs, roller blades, for example.

Confidence
1. Employ strategies to develop pupils' self-esteem (see Chapter 5), set achievable tasks, give them lots of responsibility and encouragement.
2. Focus on and only comment on positive improvements, forget the past.
3. Teach the pupil positive statements about themselves:
   One thing my friends like me for is . . .
   Something I succeeded in recently was . . .
   One of my happiest memories is . . .
   One thing I like about myself is . . .
4. Daily self-esteem programme: tell some good news, have some fun, listen to uplifting music, do some exercise, set a realistic target.
5. Teach/show another pupil a skill.

Control

1. Openly discuss your concerns with the pupil and establish a contract for them to complete small achievable amounts of work, to fixed deadlines. Establish short term achievable goals and gradually increase.
2. Vary activities, introduce the unexpected into lessons. Involve the pupil in contributing and determining the nature of the learning programme.
3. Set up positive contracts with agreed positive and negative consequences.
4. Give the pupil a card with specific instruction on to follow in difficult situations.
5. Teach the pupil thought stopping techniques. For example, 'whenever I think I'm being left out, I will go and ask one of my buddies if I can join in their game'.

Patience

1. Develop very structured lessons, and clear and explicit goals.
2. Develop a range of Intentional Statements, for example, 'Today I will . . .'.
3. Encourage pupils to breathe calmly and talk positively to themselves when in a hurry. For example, 'I have been here before, I can cope with this.'
4. Encourage pupils to complete monotonous tasks. For example, crossing out all the 'e's on a page of writing; adding up in threes for five minutes.
5. Imagery: Help pupils picture themselves doing the things they want to do. Ask them to see how they are standing, what they are saying, rehearse them acting as they want to in their mind's eye.

Relationships

1. Let pupils know that you believe in them and have confidence in them being able to do better.
2. Involve pupils in cooperative learning projects. Set the group an objective with a group reward available only when each member has completed their part.
3. Pair pupils with a peer for peer teaching or tutoring. Can they help others in an area of strength or an area of development?
4. Use team teaching, the variety of approaches can stimulate interest, or the pupil may relate better with one person than another.
5. Check pupils' understanding of friendship skills, and teach or set them homework of practising certain aspects of friendship skills.

Achievement

1. Set aside protected time in class for the pupil to complete any unfinished work.
2. Negotiate an agreed amount of work to be completed in a set time for a set reward.
3. Find an area of interest or ability and set assignments related to it.
4. Use alternative teaching methods. For example, simulation exercises.
5. Catch the pupil achieving in a wide range of situations. For example, playing well during break time, asking for help, lending a friend a pencil, listening to a story, sitting quietly.

Key points

1. Motivation decribes a pupil behaviour, it does not explain it.
2. Many pupils who are described as lacking motivation seem highly motivated to avoid work.
3. Most under-achieving pupils face barriers to their learning.
4. Success is the most powerful tool for supporting under-achieving pupils.
5. Through analysing the barriers to learning, individual programmes can be designed.

7 Listening to Children

There will be times when, much as we wish to help a distressed child, we worry whether we are doing the right thing. Should I ask questions? Will talking about it make matters worse? Should I give them a cuddle? The answer to these questions is, 'It depends'. This chapter considers some key ideas and skills that can help us get it right more often. Much of what follows is common sense. If we make a mistake we should take comfort by remembering that our intentions are good. Because listening to an emotionally troubled child is an art there are no hard and fast rules.

Emotionally troubled children often are easily hurt, have a low self-esteem, and are emotionally volatile. Some of the children we wish to support will have lost trust in adults. They will resist our attempts to get close to them. What a child seems most frightened of, or seems to avoid the most, is often what they most want. The 'I don't care' attitude often masks a need for care. It is safer for children who are used to being rejected to reject others; it protects them from further pain.

When we talk with children who are emotionally vulnerable, language can only go so far in crossing the gap between us. Words do not and never can capture the real depth of feelings that we each experience. We struggle to find words to convey our feelings. Sometimes all we can do is acknowledge children's distress and be with them. Thankfully children have a 'short sadness span'. This means that while powerful emotions will be experienced they do not stay with the child constantly. In the classroom for much of the time a vulnerable child is responding as any other child. But then strong emotions can flow and the child's behaviour changes immediately. These processes are not happening at a conscious level. They are in response to inner processes that be triggered by outside events.

For example, a child has a pencil taken by a peer. Normally they would complain and make a fuss, but this time their response is fuelled by the anger they carry through being hurt and neglected at home. Their response is now an aggressive lashing out with fists.

Because we are working with children with emotional difficulties we need to be aware of how emotions can be expressed. A child's behaviour can provide key information as to what they are experiencing within. We need to be observant and then look for the emotional logic that pushes a child to behave in such a way. The behaviour we observe is ambiguous and the same behaviour can reflect different emotions. For example, the aggressive child may in fact be depressed, but the emotional energy is being turned into a more acceptable emotion for the child to face. Many of our children with challenging behaviour are reflecting their disturbed inner world. To exclude such children from school is the last thing they need. While schools are not designed to be therapeutic there is much we can do to help unhappy and troubled children.

Understanding the emotions behind the behaviour

We have already looked at defence mechanisms and how they can protect children from experiencing painful emotions. Now we need to look at what lies behind many of the difficult behaviours children display when emotionally troubled. In the diagram (Figure 7.1) the behaviours are presented in the rectangles and the possible emotional reasons in the triangles.

Listening

Much has been written about listening effectively. Figure 7.2 can serve as an aide-mémoire of the key skills involved. Most teachers probably use many of these skills unthinkingly, but be open to new ideas that can help you support a child more.

Working with children's emotions

While we will often sit and talk with children about their worries there are other equally helpful ways to support children who are facing difficult times. There will also be some children who find it extremely difficult to explain what they are feeling or even to understand our efforts to speak with them. (Children with learning disabilities, mild or severe, will have the same emotions but lack the words to understand and describe their inner world.)

Emotions need to be experienced to prevent them being suppressed or turned in on the child in a negative way. Remember that emotions are normal healthy reactions to life experiences. They become negative and harmful for various reasons. Some emotions may be too frightening for children to face or perhaps they feel these emotions will not be accepted by the adults who care for them. Children may also fear the consequences and/or embarrassment of expressing certain emotions. Negative emotions that are not expressed will find ways of being released. Anger may be expressed in over the top reactions to everyday frustrations, persistent sadness may prevail at the loss of a possession.

Children express their feelings in a range of ways. What we are looking for are ways in which a child's painful emotions can be safely expressed. As adults we can find ourselves in tears when watching a film because it has touched an emotionally charged aspect of our lives. For example, I can feel sad when watching *Lassie Come Home*, the reason being that it touches on an unresolved aspect of loss in my own life. The emotions that we try to avoid expressing remain with us and will leak out in a whole range of ways. Sometimes the way in which we speak or stand reflects our inner feelings more than we appreciate.

Here are some ideas for helping children who may not be able to, or even wish to, share the emotions they are experiencing.

1. **Creative work (passive)** such as stories, poems, films, plays. There are many stories that allow children to deal with sensitive issues 'one remove from themselves'. This can make it easier to face and safer. (This is in the same vein as when we ask for help on behalf of a friend. The friend is really us.)

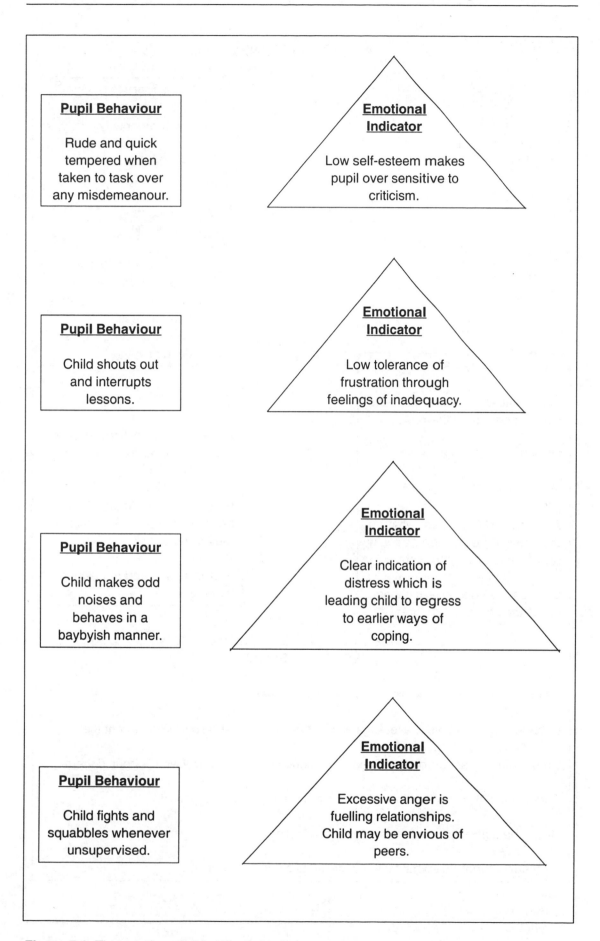

Figure 7.1 The emotions behind the behaviour

A GOOD LISTENER

LISTENS WITH FULL ATTENTION

listen with your ears
I HEAR YOUR

listen with your eyes
I SEE YOU

listen with your mind
I UNDERSTAND YOU

listen with your heart
I AM WITH YOU

UNDERSTANDS SILENCES
as another way of saying

I am frightened
It's too painful to tell you
I am embarrassed
I am confused
I am thinking
I don't like you
I feel weak if I tell you
I don't understand
I fear the consequences
I am protecting myself
I am protecting others
I can't explain

TALKS

In sentences no more than 3–5 words longer than the child's.

Uses the child's own words.

Rephrases difficult questions.

Asks the child to repeat what they have agreed to do as a way of checking understanding.

Enables the child to teach them about their own world.

PROVIDES INFORMATION

Answers the questions that are asked, not the ones they feel should be asked.

Provides honest information, and doesn't pretend to have all the answers.

Acts in a calm and reassuring manner.

RESPECTS FEELINGS

Treats broken feelings as seriously as broken bones.

Respects and accepts the feelings a child has, not 'You shouldn't worry about that'.

Understands that irrational feelings make sense when you know what's behind them.

Gives 'them' their wishes through fantasy, 'I wish it hadn't happened.'

Helps them find the words to express their feelings.

Reassures them that what they are feeling is a normal reaction.

Figure 7.2 Listening skills

2. **Creative work (active)** such as painting, pottery, singing, drama, dancing. Any expressive activity will enable emotions to find a pathway. Children will not necessarily realise what they are doing, but if they become genuinely involved with such an activity then their emotions are bound to become involved and expressed.

3. **Exercise** such as running, gymnastics, swimming, football, netball. For some children the stress that they are experiencing will result in physical tension as their bodies are switched onto a fight or flight reaction. At such times some form of physical exercise can be especially of value.

4. **Relaxation** such as breathing, muscle relaxation, guided imagery. While trying to help children express their emotions and accept them as normal reactions there can be times when we will want to help a child take control of them. The child who is quickly switched into a strong emotional reaction because of some outside cue is in danger of becoming over controlled by such an emotion. Excessive expression of an emotion can become habitual. The original reason for the emotion may have past, but the emotion remains. An example could be anger. A boy has experienced anger on account of one of his parents leaving his home. The anger is displaced onto peers through frequent fights. The boy learns to respond to any conflict with aggression. The rush of adrenalin that accompanies the aggression is stimulating. The boy has come to terms with his family break-up but remains aggressive. Our task in such situations where we feel this has happened is to help the child learn techniques that can block such emotional responses. (See Chapter 11, Anger Management.)

Confidentiality

Children may give us information that suggests or indicates that they or others may be in real danger. At such times it is our responsibility to inform other relevant agencies. The school may have a named Child Protection Officer who will need to be informed. At such times it may seem that we are betraying the confidence a child has in us. But the safety of the child or other persons must be paramount. We need to convey to the child our continuing support to them when such circumstances occur. This can be done by using the following explanations (you would naturally change the wording to reflect your own style):

What goes on in these meetings is private, between you and me only.

This means that we won't gossip to people who 'don't need to know'.

But if something is said which means 'you' or somebody else is in some sort of danger, and needs protecting – then I will speak to those people 'who need to know'.

I will explain to you who I will have to see and why.

'I will stay with you throughout.'

When to refer on or seek advice

There will also be times when we feel 'out of our depth' or have other concerns that justify involving more specialist help. Referring on needs to be seen as a strength not a weakness. It is foolhardy to pretend that we are able to help all children who turn to us.

You should always seek support if a child's reaction to an event seems severer than one would expect; when a child's reaction lasts longer than one might expect; or when the reaction is not what one expects for the age and gender of the child.

Sensitive relationships

It will be a sad day when an adult thinks twice about physically comforting a child in distress. Nevertheless, we need to be sure of our reasons. Not all children like being hugged; sadly, for some it will stir painful memories. The aim of a hug or gentle hand on the arm should be to console the child.

Some of the children we are supporting may behave towards us through sexualised behaviour. With such children we should consider supporting them with a colleague involved and avoid isolated rooms. This will change the dynamics of the relationship and agreed ways of behaving can be established. There can be times when one-to-one relationships are best avoided if the child is to be supported as positively and sensitively as possible.

Interview techniques

When interviewing children use short sentences, no more than three to five words longer than the child's sentences; use child's words and names rather than pronouns; avoid asking 'do you understand', rather ask the child to repeat your message. Do not repeat questions the child didn't understand, but rephrase them.

The physical context needs to be unthreatening. The ideal place to conduct an interview is in an uncluttered carpeted room which is not too large, furnished with adjacent low and comfortable chairs. Equip the room with appropriate age toys, puppets and writing and drawing materials. Allow the child to sit near the door.

Some children will find it easier to talk if they have a friend with them. Never forget to ask children how they would like to be supported. There is no one correct way, the aim is to find out what will best suit the child you are with.

Developing children's coping skills

Children face challenges at home and at school, that is a fact of life. Our aim is to try to improve how children deal with their challenges.

Information
Provide clear, simple, specific information prior to any event that you believe or feel will cause upset and worry, or as soon afterwards as possible. This can both help reduce anticipatory anxiety and prevent children producing incorrect explanations (misattribution).

Ventilation
Some children will feel that they are meant to be brave and hold back their feelings. Give them permission to express their anger or sadness. This will help them to master the situation and prevent them suppressing their feelings.

Rituals
If the child is suffering specific distress such as bereavement or loss it helps to involve them in developing rituals around the event. For example, a child might care for a flower bed that was planted in memory of a parent, teacher or friend. Such activities help children develop control and strengthen their own personal sense of confidence in being able to cope.

Solutions

By the age of four or five children are able to produce their own alternative solutions to the problems they face. Involve them in finding solutions to their own difficulties.

Understanding skills

There will be times when our aim is to help children make sense of what has happened to them. We may suspect 'faulty thinking', where children blame themselves, or they may have no understanding as to why they feel as they do. They may habitually rely on defence mechanisms, blaming others for an argument that they were equally responsible for. Figure 7.3 offers some useful phrases for developing different kinds of understanding.

Children with specific challenges

In all schools there are some children who have to face particularly challenging situations. There will be children who have suffered physical injury through accidents or who have life threatening conditions, such as cancer or heart conditions, which require operations. Almost certainly there will be those who bear the burden of asthma or diabetes and need ongoing medical care. Some children may have sensory impairments and need equipment to access information; others may have learning difficulties or communication difficulties.

It is not unusual to hear comments about the courage and strength of such children to cope with their school life: 'You wouldn't know they had such a problem.' We must be watchful and aware that such apparent 'normality' masks incredible internal pressure to live up to an inappropriate standard.

Any sudden change in children's lives will cause change within them that will take both time and energy to come to terms with. If the change is brought about by an illness or accident there will be a loss of control. Any loss will trigger reactions best understood through the grieving process but equally applicable here:

METHODS	AIMS	EXAMPLE PHRASES
Attribution	To help the pupil make sense of the difficulty	It seems as if you are blaming yourself . . . Do you see it like this?
Interpretation	To offer alternative explanations that give them new meaning	From what you have said, you seem to be very worried for your friend. Is that a fair comment?
Caring confrontation	To expand their awareness into areas that they may find painful to explore	While you are saying that on the one hand you want to . . . on the other hand you are also saying . . .
Problem clarification	To clarify difficulties and begin to set goals	Can you give me some specific examples of this?

Figure 7.3 Understanding skills

- shock (causing confusion of what to do);
- denial (not being able to accept the new situation);
- anger (why me?);
- sorrow (at the loss of something of value).

As children move in and out of these reactions we see that some will pass through the process quickly, others will take much longer: there is no right or wrong length of time. Some will return to different stages of the process, and then go forward again. Grief is a healing process that takes time and emotional energy, and there will be times when children have less energy for learning than they normally would.

To get to the point where most children start, children with specific challenges have to make great effort. Even before they arrive in school some will have faced additional struggles – of doing buttons up, of knowing they wet the bed, of knowing that other people find their speech difficult to understand. And what about children who face learning difficulties? The following poignant and true anecdote shows the pain they can feel.

A father had just finished reading a story to his daughter – who was having difficulties with reading. Instead of looking happy she seemed sad. 'Why the glum look?' he asked. The little girl explained that she was sad because she much enjoyed him reading to her but this was something she would not be able to do for her own children.

Most children do not have to face these experiences but children with such challenges will draw on their emotional energy to cope – or overcome, or accept, or get angry – with their experiences. When you add up all the 'little challenges' that some children will face over and above those we take for granted as being part of normal everyday life, then it is clear that they will need extra help.

It is hard to imagine how it must be for children who are to have a serious heart operation. They do not need to be told how worried their parents are for them: they can see it in their faces. Such a worry will take energy from the child. Their day is heavier than ours. Like adults, they will sometimes seem preoccupied. In class occasional reminders will draw them to the forthcoming trip to the hospital and create a distraction from learning.

For children in a wheelchair coping so well, the biggest challenge is not physically getting into school but being enveloped in sympathy and sadness by the adults who meet them. Try to imagine yourself as that child in a wheelchair: every time you meet new people you see the look on their face that says what a shame, how sad, how do they cope. Some young people face that each day and have to cope with it somehow. To face it takes emotional energy, to avoid it takes emotional energy. Emotional energy is taken from the child, energy that is not available for learning and having fun.

As a result of the negative messages, often implicit and masked by care and sympathy, some children come to struggle with the wish 'that they were not who they are'. This is particularly true for adolescents. Children with challenges will try to appear normal, as if there were no problem, at the cost of considerable effort.

What can be done? They will benefit from:

- your and their own awareness of their rights to equal opportunities;
- focused care and support of their self-esteem;
- being taught relaxation skills;
- being given positive self statements;
- being given assertiveness training;
- being given permission not to have to make the effort all the time;

- being involved in improving their environment;
- being given choice and control.

They will also benefit if teachers actively address issues which affect their situation; for instance, by challenging institutional discrimination (where are the ramps? why are there so few wheelchair users in schools? where are the books that show people with disabilities to be like anyone else?); putting equal opportunity issues into the curriculum; displaying and discussing the achievements of differently abled people as much as others; inviting differently abled people in to talk to children; using books, films and other material that reflect the fullest inclusion of differently abled people into all walks of life. Intentional bullying which is based in differences in learning, physical or sensory ability should be treated as if it were discrimination on gender or racial grounds. And it should be a priority of teachers to make the inclusion of differently abled children and students an equal opportunities issue and not a special needs one.

Key points

1. We can learn to understand the emotions that lie behind children's behaviour.
2. A good listener has both the intention and the necessary skills.
3. When children are distressed we can offer clear and positive support.
4. Children cope with additional challenges through using extra emotional energy.
5. Inclusion is a major educational challenge, there are many barriers to be overcome, but if you are looking for solutions, it will happen.

---

8 A Solution Focused Approach

Solution Focused Brief Therapy (SFBT) is a useful approach for special educational needs coordinators (SENCOs) and class teachers to use when helping pupils with emotional difficulties. It is called Brief Solution Focused Counselling in the USA because using the term therapy to describe 'within-school' activities is not permitted there. What we shall describe here is the use of a number of solution-focused techniques and then discuss how these could be applied to a school setting. The techniques are described within the context of a standard solution-focused interview. In real life situations the order of questioning will be determined as much by the flow of conversation between interviewer and interviewee as by the need to follow a certain structure.

Background information on SFBT

SFBT is based on the model developed by family therapists Steve de Shazer and Isoo DeBerg at the Brief Family Therapy Center in Milwaukee. John Rhodes (1993) described the development of SFBT as a drawing together of a number of influences and counselling approaches to produce 'a way of thinking which can be applied in many everyday situations from casework to consultation with organisations. It might in fact be a sort of complementary framework to the problem solving model'.

One of the first centres to develop SFBT in the UK, from 1989 onwards, was the Marlborough Family Services Centre. This is a NHS child and adult psychiatric clinic in St John's Wood, London. It serves a wide-ranging community from different ethnic and social backgrounds.

From here George, Iveson and Ratner published *Problem to Solution* (1990) and went on to establish 'the Brief Therapy Practice', which offers direct counselling as well as training over 200 professionals annually. SFBT has been applied to educational settings since 1995 and its use in such settings is described by Rhodes and Ajmal (1995). SFBT is now widely used in clinical, social services and educational settings throughout the world.

Fogell (1996) defined SFBT thus:

> Its characteristics are: clear structure; concentration on clients' strengths and capacity to imagine solutions; establishing goals clients find meaningful; rating different aspects of life to establish priorities. It helps individuals to recognise their own resources, strengths, beliefs and behaviour to achieve change in their life.

Why use SFBT in schools?

SFBT has its origins in clinical settings. In this section we are not suggesting that teachers become therapists. We are however arguing that SFBT can be adapted to the needs of schools and it provides a helpful framework for class teachers, SENCOs, SEN support teachers and educational psychologists (see Figure 8.1).

It would not be appropriate for a teacher or educational psychologist to consider entering into a long term therapeutic relationship with children or their parents. The time demands on the teacher through the myriad tasks that are involved in preparing and presenting lessons and monitoring progress make such a demand unachievable. Educational psychologists too are under considerable constraints because of the demands of the SEN procedures (DES 1994). Many would argue that building up long term relationships with families and offering a range of interventions should be within the remit of educational psychologists, and it may well be with the developments which follow the revision of the Code of Practice that such interventions become possible (DfEE 1998a).

However, for the medium term future, it is likely that there will be limited time and a variety of competing demands on teachers and the professionals who support them. SFBT gives a very useful framework for family therapy which was cited in *Excellence for All*, the 1998 Green Paper on SEN, as the sort of intervention which educational psychologists might do as a preventative measure.

It meets time demands

SFBT fits into the time frame of the educational psychologist and teacher. As the name suggests SFBT is by design brief. There is some evidence to suggest that even a single session using this approach can be helpful (Talmon 1990). Usually the process will be used to set some form of goals or objectives and therefore follow-up monitoring sessions will be helpful.

It gives quick insight

SFBT gives a quick insight into concerns of pupils, parents and teachers focusing on areas of success. It is theoretically possible for a counsellor to use SFBT to good effect without any discussion of the problems concerning the child or parent. Inevitably the children, parents or teachers will often be eager to discuss their concerns and will derive some comfort from the fact that their problem is understood. In SFBT, however, the problem is less important than the features of the solution. Whilst avoiding any suggestion that the problem is unimportant, the counsellor using SFBT will quickly move the discussion on to explore the indicators of progress and the feature of non-problem times which are familiar to the child, parent or teacher.

It increases empowerment

SFBT increases empowerment for pupils, parents and teachers. Throughout the process of counselling using SFBT the aim is to identify those things which will tell clients that they are making progress or how they will know that things are getting better. It is therefore essentially geared to increase the individual's capacity to recognise and develop new coping skills and strategies.

Solution Focused Individual Behaviour Programme Planning Sheet

Throughout this process seek maximum involvement of the child. The more they own the solutions and targets the more likely they will be to work hard to achieve the targets.

➤ Step 1:   In column A (sheet 2) list up to five problems you wish to work on.

➤ Step 2:   In column B list a corresponding solution to each problem, i.e. what you want the child to do instead of the problem behaviour

➤ Step 3:   Fold the paper along the line A–B.

➤ Step 4:   Tear the paper along the fold and discard column A.

➤ Step 5:   Select the three solutions towards which the child is most likely to make early progress.

➤ Step 6:   Estimate the child's progress to date towards the solution on a scale from 1=no progress noted, to 10=solution goal reached

Solution 1	1	2	3	4	5	6	7	8	9	10
Solution 2	1	2	3	4	5	6	7	8	9	10
Solution 3	1	2	3	4	5	6	7	8	9	10

➤ Step 7:   Think about the things that tell you the child has reached his/her current point on the scale (look for even the smallest indicators).

➤ Step 8:   List as short term targets the behaviours that will tell you the child has made the first step up the scale towards their goal.

Target 1	
Target 2	
Target 3	

➤ Step 9:   List those things that you can do to help the child reach the targets:

_____

_____

_____

_____

Figure 8.1 Solution focused individual behaviour planning sheet

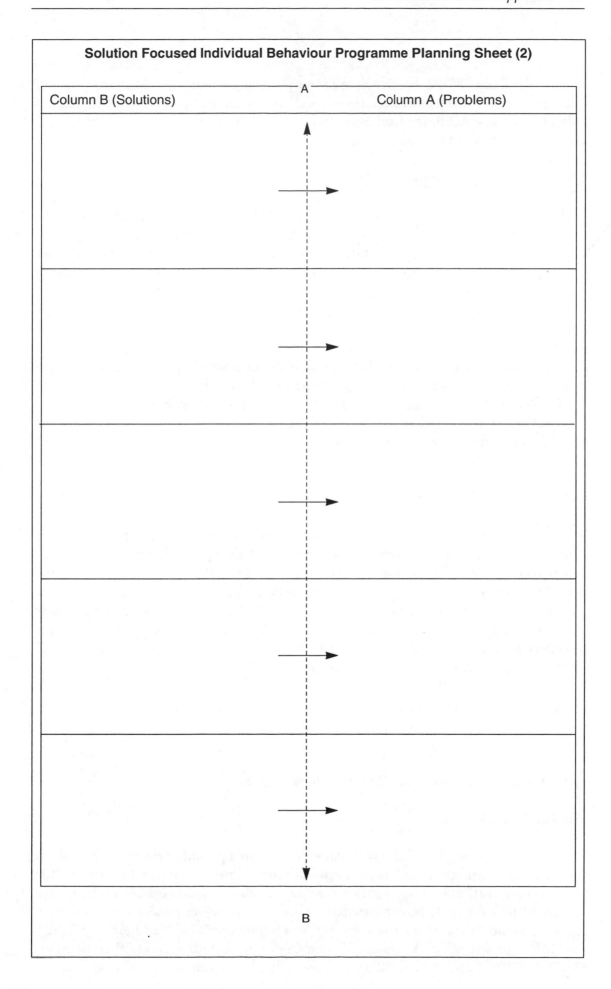

It identifies solutions

The essential aim of the process is to identify solutions that are within the grasp of individuals. They may have become focused on problems that are hindering them. It helps to evaluate solutions from the perspective of others that are close to the client and avoids setting unrealistic goals.

It sets priorities

Problem solving can be a complex process involving a number of steps. One of the most important aspects of overcoming problems is experiencing early success. This helps to boost confidence and motivates individuals to continue their efforts. SFBT helps clients to work on those targets that are within their grasp and therefore increases the likelihood of early success.

It makes evaluation easier

SFBT gives success criteria to make evaluation of effectiveness easier. Each discussion using SFBT is likely to result in some exploration of objectives or progress indicators. As the recipients become more sophisticated in the process they become better able to set reachable targets and better able to identify progress, and they quickly become able to do it without counselling support.

Counselling ground rules

A counselling relationship, whether it is between a class teacher and pupil or a professional counsellor and client, should follow clear ground rules. Rule number one is that participants should receive a non-conditional positive regard from the counsellor (people are less likely to talk honestly and openly to those they think are sitting in judgement on, or disapprove of, them). Other important principles are: confidentiality (usual caveats apply, i.e. child protection issues); empowering; uninterrupted agreed time given; empathy and warmth; honesty and openness.
   Three further ground rules are characteristic of SFBT:
If it ain't broke don't fix it.
Once you know what works do more of it.
If it doesn't work, don't do it again. Do something different.

Techniques for a standard SFBT interview

Problem free talk

A conversation using SFBT should ideally begin with a period of problem free talk. It is easy to dash straight to talk of the issues of concern but it is helpful to spend a little time in conversation before embarking on the substance of the session. Problem free talk enables a rapport to be established or a link with previous sessions. It transmits a sense of value to the child (they are not just a problem) and can help to identify motivators or strengths. A context of competence is created, showing that the interviewer is relaxed and can take the interview in their own time.

Goal setting

Throughout any conversation there will be opportunity to set goals. Starting off a conversation with the question 'How will you know at the end of this session whether it was worthwhile coming?' enables the interviewer to be mindful throughout of the concerns and aspirations of the child, parent or teacher.

Goals need to be clear; be set by the client; and include observable indications of change.

Indicators of progress should identify what the client will see themselves doing and what significant others will see.

The miracle question

This is one of the most important of the techniques associated with SFBT. It helps to set goals where clients have not got clear goals of their own. The actual wording of the miracle question will vary according to the understanding of the recipient. A different wording will be appropriate with younger children. (For example, it is important to ensure that younger children know what the word miracle means.) The following is a model of the miracle question which can be adapted to different circumstances: 'Imagine that after you have gone to bed tonight, whilst you are sleeping, a miracle happens and the problems that brought you here today are resolved. You don't know it's happened because you are asleep. When you wake up in the morning, how will you know the miracle has happened?'

Other person perspective

When using the miracle question or when goal setting it is helpful to ask how others would tell if change occurred. What will indicate to other family members that progress is being made? How will friends know that the problem is gone, what will they see you doing that is different? How will your colleagues tell that you have reached your objectives?

Problems are usually multi-causal and therefore solutions should be multi-faceted. By reflecting on what other people will see, the solutions described can be evaluated more thoroughly. This helps to avoid those solutions suggested in conversation from becoming future problems.

Exception finding

Sometimes it is important for the children, parents or teachers to discuss their concerns. Part of building up empathy in any therapeutic relationship involves understanding the background to the worries.

When discussing problems it can help to find out those times or circumstances when the problem is not evident. Exploring times when the problem is less intrusive can also help.

Imagine the child saying that they are getting bullied in school. By asking: 'When was the last time in school when that didn't happen?' the counsellor can explore:

- when is the child safer;
- which other pupils are most likely to be a source of support to the child;
- which teachers can most effectively deal with the bullies;
- what triggers off the bullies;

● what behaviour is likely to be helpful in avoiding or responding to situations when bullying may occur.

The circumstances surrounding exceptions can be a good source of strengths on which to build in future.

Scaling

Scaling questions can be introduced early into the conversation.
'On a scale of one to ten, with one being the worst that things have been and ten representing how you want things to be, where are you now?'
'So what is it that tells you that you have moved from one to . . .?' (This helps to identify current strengths that the interviewee might be unaware of.)
'What would be a reasonable position to aim for next?'
'How will you know when you have got there?'

Locating resources

The aim of SFBT is to help clients to identify their personal resources to work towards solutions. In discussing the resources available to the pupil, parent or teacher false or inappropriate goals can be avoided. For an attendance problem, it may help to state a goal of: 'The child will be maintaining full school attendance'.

If the parents do not have sufficient ability to ensure the child goes to school each day then the goal will not be achieved. Perhaps a more appropriate goal would be that everybody is giving a consistent message that it is really important for the child to be attending school every day. Once that has been achieved then the next step may be locating resources within the school to help draw the child into school, such as peers' support, the educational welfare officer, a classroom support assistant. Some helpful questions are:
How have they dealt with this sort of problem in the past?
How have they shown personal strengths in the past?
How have they shown creative problem solving?
Who are the most significant people they can draw support from?

Coping

Sometimes it is not possible to identify times when problems have been overcome in the past. This is more likely with children who have fewer life experiences. Exploring how the client copes with the problem currently can identify strengths. Such questions need to be conveyed in a genuine spirit of enquiry to avoid clients inferring that their problem is regarded as minor and that it is not being taken seriously.

Stopping things getting worse

Sometimes children, their parents or teachers cannot identify meaningful exceptions. It is possible that they cannot accept the idea that they are coping. Indeed, in some circumstances, if a child is a victim of abuse or the family is coping with debt or other difficult life circumstances, the short term discussion should focus on strategies to stop things getting worse.

If the client appears to be unable to make progress it may be indicative of more serious difficulties. Whenever a problem persists despite detailed support it is important to consider the possibility of calling on additional support. In our last book (Fogell and Long 1996) we gave a simple rule of thumb: If in doubt, make a referral.

Discussion with the educational psychologist may be appropriate to refine an Individual Behaviour support programme.

The Child and Adolescent Mental Health Services (CAMHS) would be appropriate if parents are reporting serious difficulties in the home. The Social Services Department may be appropriate if the child is experiencing life circumstances that nobody should be expected to endure.

Constructive feedback

Throughout each session it is important to highlight anything which might contribute to clients reaching their goal, for example: attitude during the session; responses from other people; comments they make; and evidence of determination, perseverance, creative thinking.

All sessions should end with a constructive summary. The end of a conversation is very important. Often the discussions held using a SFBT are complex and can draw out a range of issues. It can help to leave the room to reflect for five minutes before returning to summarise.

Ending

The ending of a SFBT session can be the key to starting the next session constructively. The following points can help to make the ends of sessions smooth, positive and effective:

- end the session close to the time allotted;
- if unforeseen items are raised close to the time for ending agree to discuss them at a future date;
- refer to the goals stated at the start of the session;
- remind the client of the indicators of progress.

One favourite SFBT final comment is 'Watch out for the miracle happening!' When individuals have become accustomed to a problem they may fail to notice small changes which indicate progress. By referring them to the things they described in the miracle question they can be encouraged to spot those positive times in their life. This can help to boost confidence and motivation and is as valid for setting learning goals as in any other areas.

Professional goal setting

SFBT can be used by professionals to self monitor their progress towards goals. Any project or professional concern can be approached in this way. Think of a professional issue and go through the following questions in relation to it:

- How will you know when things are going as you want them to? (Perhaps use the miracle question.)
- Scale your current concern. On a scale of one to ten – if one was the point at which you were most concerned, or starting the project, and ten is the end of the project, or when you have no concerns – where are you now?
- Identify progress. If you have made progress what tells you so? What does that tell you about your potential for change?

- If no progress has been made refer to the miracle question then try to identify first realistic steps towards your miracle.
- Identify resources, personal, within your workplace.
- Set a realistic target. What will be good enough progress?
- Identify success criteria.

SFBT: a short case study

Tom was experiencing lots of problems in school. He was missing lessons, turning up to lessons without the correct equipment, arriving at the SEN department saying he was unhappy and had left his class, not handing in homework, arriving late for school. Tom's teacher called his parents in to discuss the situation. Tom had lived for most of his childhood with his paternal grandparents. His mother had died when he was an infant school child. Tom's father lived with his partner, Edith, and there was little love lost between her and Tom's grandparents. Recently Tom had moved to live with his father and Edith because his grandparents had retired to their house in France. Both Tom and his father had severe specific learning difficulties. Edith, on the other hand, loved books and was an avid reader. When Edith and Tom's dad went in to school they reported that they could do nothing with him. He was: lazy, untidy, argumentative and spent lots of time in his room. Dad was supportive but found it difficult to work with school because of his own bad experiences as a young person. Tom was referred to the educational psychology service as a result of the discussions that had taken place between Tom, his father, step-mother and teacher. All four had indicated that they wanted to make a change in the current situation. I decided to work with Tom, Edith and his support teacher using a SFBT approach to try to develop a more positive relationship between Tom and his significant adults. It is not possible to detail all of the process of discussion. By working with all three the following outcomes were achieved in two SFBT sessions:

- Tom's teachers all reported that he was making better progress in class. Tom was able to explain that he found talking through his problems difficult because he often did not understand the questions put to him by adults.
- Edith was able to understand that some of the things Tom did, which seemed problematic to her, were done because Tom felt they were helpful.
- Both Tom and Edith were able to make a commitment to work towards getting on better.
- Edith felt less to blame for Tom's difficulties and established a very supportive relationship with Tom's teachers.
- Tom's teacher was able to point out to him that relying less on her was progress.
- Edith was able to understand that Tom's reluctance to read was for a very good reason.

Tom and Edith both asked for a third counselling session because they had found the process to be helpful but then said they were able to negotiate their relationship from that time onwards.

Figure 8.2 shows one evaluation of progress using the professional monitoring sheet.

Solution Focused Brief Therapy planner

Details of the Project/Casework   Date: 6th April 1998
Casework involving Tom Glass

Who/What is involved in this process?
Tom Glass (Pupil);   Edith Weaver (Step-mum);   Sharon Plessy (Support Teacher);
Jonathan A Fogell (Educational Psychologist)

How will you know when things are going as you want them to?
Tom will be reporting that things are going well at home. Edith will report that she feels that
Tom and she are getting on together.

Scale your current concern
Problem at   1   2   3   4   5   6   7   8   9   10   Problem
its worst   has gone

Indicators of progress so far
1. Edith reports that Tom has made an effort to be more tidy.   2. Tom reported that he
has had some chats with Edith.   3. Tom and his Dad have done some DIY work together
(laying concrete).

If no progress has been made so far use the 'miracle question'   N/A

Identify resources, personal, within your workplace
Edith and Tom both relate well to the teacher who asked for SFBT intervention. Both Tom
and Edith have talked openly about their concerns and have made clear statements that
they want to get on together. Both Tom and Edith have been prepared to listen to each
other's point of view. Edith is becoming increasingly aware of Tom's reading difficulties
and able to acknowledge other talents and skills that he has. Tom now accepts that Edith
has a right to be happy and contented and he can contribute to her happiness with only
small modifications to his life.

Set a realistic target based on 'good enough' progress
Tom will continue to make better progress in school. Tom to be better organised in school.
Edith will feel that Tom is making an effort to talk with her.

Identify success criteria
1. Tom will complete homework at the homework club before going home.   2. Edith and
Tom will eat evening meal together and chat about the day.   3. Tom will only attend the
SEN room for a chat once per day.

Date of Next Review   5th May 1998

Figure 8.2 Solution Focused Brief Therapy planner

Selective mutism

One way of comparing the difference in emphasis between a problem focused approach and a solution focused approach is by applying each approach to a particular problem. Selective (or elective) mutism provides one such example. This is a relatively rare condition characterised by a consistent failure to speak in specific social situations in which there is an expectation for speaking, and it can often be confused with excessive shyness.

Children with selective mutism have the ability to both speak and understand language, but choose not to use this ability. It is therefore not a language disorder. In adults selective mutism would be regarded as a social phobia/social anxiety. Most children with selective mutism function normally in other areas of their lives. Selective mutism is not a communications disorder and is not part of a developmental disorder. By definition, selective mutism does not include children with conduct disorders, oppositional/defiant behaviour, and/or attention-deficit hyperactivity disorder.

The principal problem in children with selective mutism appears to be anxiety (causing avoidance behaviour). However, children who do not speak in 'normal' situations can appear to be very powerful. Treatment of selective mutism can result in frustrations because of the apparent resistance to adult intervention

Using a problem focused approach

Herbert (1991) describes the principles which may be adopted in a problem focused approach:

> Carry out a functional analysis of the problem focusing on the situations and the people involved when the child currently speaks.

> Carry out an analysis of the verbal interaction in the classroom. Point out how current verbal interaction may reinforce the child's non-communication.

> Use situation fading by systematically rewarding small efforts at talking as the child is moved gradually from situations where they currently talk to a situation where they currently don't talk.

> Provide extrinsic motivators contingent on the child showing approximations to speaking behaviour.

> Develop a progressive schedule of behavioural objectives and systematically reward progress towards the goals e.g.
> Giving eye contact
> Playing alongside other children
> Pointing at objects on request
> Playing simple interactional games
> Responding with single words
> Making two or three word utterances
> Speaking appropriate to age and social demands of the classroom.

A solution focused approach

This approach would certainly involve accepting the child's right not to speak. Initially it would probably involve working with the people who most want to see a change in the current situation, such as parents, siblings, teachers.

A 'mandated child' may be expressing mutism as one form of resistance. Instead of problem free talk some silent activity could be used to build a rapport: a long silent walk together, watching some silent movies or looking at images without sound.

Work with parents, siblings and teachers to establish early goals using the miracle question and scaling questions. One aim might be to help this family/school whether the boy talks or stays silent. All this should be done in the presence of the child, saying you are perfectly comfortable hearing only the other's side. State clearly that it is not the child's responsibility to talk with you and that it is okay to remain silent. Acknowledge the co-operation shown in coming to you. If this pupil is so resistant why does he show up?

Acknowledge the success of the parents, peers or teachers involved in getting the pupil to show up for counselling. Give positive feedback to the pupil about his progress as reported to you by others.

Explore exceptions to the problem. When is the child talking? What is different about those times? Maybe there is a friend with whom the pupil has talked in the past: could the friend be invited to join in a session? Empathise with the pupil by telling him it must be tough for him to have other people worrying about him. One future target might be that other people are less worried about him. This could be done using a visual cue:

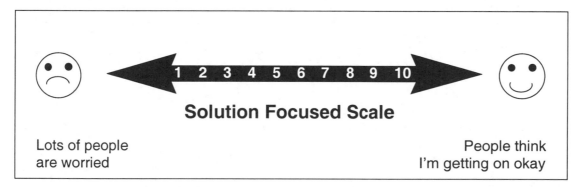

Then put the following questions:

1. Where would you place yourself on the above scale?
2. Where would be a reasonable place to aim for?
3. How will you know when you have got there? (written response)

Another line of questioning would relate to how the pupil is coping with the current problem. How are family members, peers, and teacher coping?

Sessions should end with a summary of the strengths and positives that have been identified in the session, and the goals that have been identified. The focus child should be encouraged to signal if he disagrees with any of the summary points. In this way he can be encouraged to take ownership of the targets and to be enlisted in the process of working towards the solution.

Summary

SFBT gives a clear structure to a counselling approach which can be applied to a variety of problems. It maintains a positive focus, allows the professional to help in attaining goals that will be meaningful to the recipient, and gives a framework for evaluation that can be passed on to other professionals in complex cases

More information on SFBT may be had through the Brief Therapy Practice and other course providers; the LEA Educational Psychology Service; Child and Adolescent Mental Health Services.

A range of publications on SFBT is now available, for instance: Furman (1999); O'Connell (1999); Stringer and Mall (1999).

Key points

1. SFBT emphasises children's strengths.
2. For SFBT, understanding the solution is more important than understanding the problem.
3. SFBT helps us to find those exceptions when the problem does not occur, and to increase their chance of happening.
4. Because it is brief SFBT is an ideal strategy for school staff.
5. SFBT enables everyone to see the smallest sign of improvement.

---

9 Loss and Separation

Sadness in children is a normal but debilitating emotion. It has a healthy and an unhealthy side. When it is associated with loss it can be part of the painful but normal healing process. But when it is tied to failure and purposelessness it is very negative. Like adults, some children will be more vulnerable to this emotion than others. This may be through temperamental disposition and/or early experiences. Like any other emotion sadness has its own dynamics. Once children are in the grips of sadness they are more likely to experience negative experiences. For many children today their sadness will be in reaction either to the loss of a parent through death or to family breakdown. Whichever it is, the more we understand the better able we will be to give the best support and care we can.

Bereavement

Statistics reveal that 180,000 children in the UK under 16 have experienced the death of a parent.

In the past adults often tried to protect children from the pain caused from bereavement. For instance, children were prevented from attending the funeral and the loved one was rarely talked about in front of them. But reminders are always there. Even the fact that the name of a loved one is never mentioned may be a reminder, or the realisation that only one ticket is needed for the school Christmas show.

The reasons why our society has treated death as a taboo topic are many and complex. It emerged as a taboo this century. In the Victorian era, death was much more a part of everyday experiences. There were family rituals to support people through their grief. With improvements in medicine and health care death became a stranger to us, and consequently all the more frightening: when it happened it was a sign of medical failure. Thankfully, through the work of such groups as the Hospice Movement, we have come a long way.

How children understand death

As children mature they change in their understanding of death. The following are some common patterns according to age:

Age 3–5 years
For the very young the word 'dead' is similar to away or gone. Death is like a temporary state of affairs, it is not final and people can be brought back. There will be emotional distress reactions of separation without the understanding of loss. At this age, children are very egocentric and can have feelings of guilt and anger. For example, 'Granny died because I didn't visit her'. Provided children have someone else they are attached to, the effect of loss may be minimised.

Age 5–9 years

At this period loss is seen as something external, for example 'an old man', 'a skeleton'. Children now will try to outsmart death – the more you know about it the less frightened you are of it. It is not unusual for children at this age to become fascinated by death and all things related, in films, toys, books and games, much to the concern of parents and teachers. They will retain some of the similarities of the previous age but now more fully appreciate the finality of death, while being ill equipped to deal with the fear and anxiety generated.

Age 9 years onwards

Children now come to see death as an end to life, that there is no coming back. They can accept that it is both universal and irreversible. Their personal values are used to make sense of life and death, and new belief systems may be explored.

Little deaths

Children are always facing 'little deaths'. These are the everyday losses, such as the loss of a best friend when the family moves away, the loss of a favourite teacher with a change of class, the loss of a pet.

When these losses occur there are always emotional reactions. We cannot be attached to somebody and then when we lose them carry on as if nothing has happened. We have to adjust to a world without the loved person or object. How children respond to these 'little deaths' will shape how they deal with the big ones. It does not help children to over protect them from such events; in fact, it makes them more vulnerable.

Attachment, loss and the grieving process

Infants quickly form an emotional bond to a mother figure. This is essential for survival. When we are with this person we feel safe and secure; when separated we are anxious and frightened. When this bond is broken we are at risk: an important biological survival bond has been broken. It is not surprising that there should be strong responses in an attempt to re-establish it. (This happens to both children and adults.) Adults search frantically when separated from their children in the supermarket. Children will cry or scream loudly for the care giver to return when they are lost. They are protesting in an angry manner.

Attachment is thus vital for our survival, but it is also the emotion which allows us to grow into loving, trusting and caring adults.

When a child experiences the death of a loved one then a set of natural emotional responses is triggered off. The exact nature of these responses will be influenced by such factors as:

- age of child (children under ten are most vulnerable);
- personal temperament;
- gender (studies have shown that boys respond more aggressively);
- relationship to deceased;
- nature of the loss (illness, suicide, murder);
- family and friendship networks;
- previous experience of loss;

- belief system;
- care (how children respond is influenced by the quality of care they receive; how well a remaining parent copes is a key factor).

The grieving process is often referred to as a healing pain. This may be likened to the process that occurs when we cut ourselves. The body takes time to form a scab and then a scar and finally new tissue. Over time, natural healing processes are taking place.

There are key stages that children will pass through. During each stage there are key emotions which are likely to be experienced, followed by the task (see Figure 9.1).

It is helpful if we use a 'journey' as a metaphor for the grieving process. Sometimes children will go back to where they have been. They may get stuck on a roundabout. If we think for a moment of our own losses, we can appreciate that for most of the time we cope well. But then a sudden reminder – an ache from a past memory – comes and we find we are feeling those grief pains flow through us as strongly as they ever did.

Understanding loss: the dark times

The emotions we experience during bereavement are normal natural ones. We experience anger at the death of our loved one. Often when children cry during this stage it is more of a screaming type of crying. They are calling their loved one back, protesting. At this stage the child is prone to denial. Later when they are mourning the loss their crying is much deeper, more of a sobbing. An acceptance has taken place. We cannot grieve the loss until we accept that the loved one is permanently gone.

Children need to grieve the loss of loved ones. They cannot love and not experience these painful emotions. Love would make no sense if there was not the pain of loss. When children experience the death of a close adult we can imagine them entering a dark tunnel. Their world is shattered. As adults we talk of people going to pieces. During this time the healing process is taking place. We must keep offering support to children even though there will be times when they will reject it. They may not be ready for support. Even when this happens we must keep offering support. We must work with children where they are in the grieving process, not where we think they should be.

When children are in the tunnel of grief they may display many symptoms. Remember, emotions are not rational. Children will respond unthinkingly to what they feel. Their behaviours need to be seen as part of their expression of grief.

Children's reactions to bereavement

Bereaved children react with expressions of sadness, anger and pining similar to those seen in adults who are grieving. The process, timing and pattern of responses differs through developmental influences.

	PROTEST	DESPAIR	ADJUST
EMOTIONS	Anger	Sadness	Coming to terms
BEHAVIOUR	Argumentative	Tearful	New friends/activities
TASKS	Accept loss	Experience grief	Adjust and cope

Figure 9.1 Key stages of the grieving process

Common reactions include: night fears, sadness, anger, crying, irritability, regression, behaviour changes, withdrawal, increased delinquency, poor school work, concentration difficulties, denial of loss, increased illness, separation difficulties and somatic symptoms. In fact, any sudden change in behaviour can be a response to the loss.

Children are far less able to tolerate the severe emotional pain caused through loss and will try to cope with the pain through using their defence mechanisms. We have already seen these at work, and they play an important role in protecting the child from excessive emotional pain. The most common defence mechanisms are:

- denial (through denying any pain the child will try to turn the emotion on its head and use the energy to put on a brave face);
- displacement (other less painful events may be used to release some of the real pain the child is feeling; for example, an extreme reaction to the loss of personal belongings);
- obsessional behaviours (the child has compulsive thoughts about death, makes frequent visits to the grave);
- aggressive outbursts (the child may swing between being very aggressive and defiant to acting passive, withdrawn and isolated);
- symptom substitution (the child may develop physical symptoms, loss of appetite, headaches and become a school refuser).

Whenever a child complains of physical illness always consult a doctor.

There are many ways in which children try to avoid and cope with the overwhelming pain that bereavement is causing them. While they are less able to cope with the emotions, children do have a 'short sadness span'. They will therefore experience emotions very intensely and then return to a more normal behaviour quite quickly.

Most bereaved children, but not all, are better by the end of the first year.

Supporting bereaved children in school

The general aims of support are to help children to accept the loss, express their feelings, accept their feelings as normal, and live without the loved one. They need to be given permission to grieve and to stop grieving, and help to become independent (see Figure 9.2).

This help should be freely given by supporting their experience of loss, helping them express their emotions and clarifying any distortions or misconceptions they may have about the event. They will need assistance in coping with family changes. In addition, children require help to understand a remaining parent's grief and the parent may need help to understand the grief of the child.

Understanding and supporting

When children suffer a loss they battle to regain the past, to turn the clock back. Anyone seeming to stand in their way is likely to face their anger. To help them we need to understand their thoughts and feelings. When we say, 'I feel that you are angry at the doctors and nurses, even though they tried hard to save Mum, but failed' this is a way of acknowledging their feelings as well as stating reality. Our role is not only to be a friend and supporter but also to represent reality. We try to sympathise with their wishes, but with care we can help them accept reality.

By looking sensitively at the 'stories' the children are telling us, contained in their

SOME IDEAS for HELPING
an aide-mémoire

Ask the child how they would like to be supported.
Share experiences with others (support group).
Keep in touch with the family.
Use literature, music.
Give permission to feelings.
Give time and attention.
Involve special friends.
Be mindful of special days.
Be honest with questions.
Be aware of previous bereavements.
Maintain self-esteem inputs.
Provide bolt holes.
Keep child with peers.
Be sensitive to child's beliefs.
Help child write poetry/letters to loved one.
Do picture stories.
Create a special album.
Normalise their thoughts and feelings.
Form a support circle.
Join CRUSE.
Visit church.
Make a memorial.
Write a journal account.
Attend the funeral.
Acknowledge loss with a card.

'We are healed from suffering only by
experiencing it to the full'
(Marcel Proust)

Figure 9.2 Understanding and supporting a grieving child

behaviour, we will be able to see the grieving task they are working on. Often those who are closely and emotionally involved are unable to take such a viewpoint.

As children experience the pain of grief, so they gain mastery over the loss. In our culture we often talk in euphemisms about death. Children are told someone is 'sleeping' or 'gone away'. This can hinder a child's sense of knowledge and mastery. Being open with children is painful. It is not easy as a carer to talk of their pain, when our natural response is to talk about other things to take their mind off their grief. But the feelings we avoid are the feelings that run our lives. As Shakespeare said: 'Give sorrow words, the grief that does not speak knits up the o'er wrought heart and bids it break.'

Normally children will work through their grief at their own pace. We need only to be with them, to show we care. It is usually unwise and unnecessary to force children on according to what we think they should be doing or experiencing. Our aim should be to support children from where they are. We can support them through:

- being open and honest;
- talking about good and difficult family memories;
- accepting their feelings;

- helping them write poems/stories/songs and do drawings to express their grief;
- helping them establish or going over a final goodbye;
- being a good listener, being there if needed;
- accepting all questions, without feeling the need to be able to answer all of them: 'I don't know' may often the right answer;
- offering brief but regular meetings.

Separation and divorce

While there are some similarities between bereavement and family breakdown the differences are greater. Divorce is an acceptable adult solution to the problem of an unhappy marriage, but it is rarely the preferred solution for children. In school we are faced with many sensitive issues when trying to support a pupil through such difficult and painful times.

There are many different questions for the teacher to address such as: How much should I ask the child or parents about family problems? How can I best support the child? Do I treat the child as usual or do I make concessions? If the child's behaviour changes when should I seek outside help? Do I communicate with one or both parents?

While there is no easy answer to such questions, each situation will be different. We can develop a general framework of support for children.

Emotions associated with family breakdown

Emotions associated with divorce and separation are anger, guilt, shame, embarrassment, fear, uncertainty, relief, confusion, anxiety and sadness. Children will feel a mixture of these emotions.

Children will need the reassurance that their feelings are normal responses to what they are going through. As they accept and experience these feelings, the feelings lose their power. If children avoid or deny the feelings then they remain waiting; feelings cannot be ignored and forgotten. Children can be very frightened by their feelings. They may become angry towards one parent. Children will often deny that there are problems and dream about their parents getting back together. This is not uncommon but children need help to accept this as 'a wish' and to come to terms with the reality.

Our aim in school will be to minimise the negative effect that family difficulties can have on children. There will be many questions that worry them:

- Where am I going to live?
- Will I be able to see both parents?
- Whose fault is it?
- Is there someone else involved?
- Will I stay with my brothers and sisters?
- Will I still see my relatives?
- Will there be enough money for us?
- Will I have to change schools?
- Do my parents still love me?
- Can I love both Mum and Dad?
- What will happen if one remarries?

Time is the important factor. Time must be spent explaining to them what is going on: being uncertain is not helpful for them at all. They need the time to ask questions and to be given honest answers. They need time to accept and get used to new arrangements, and time to come to terms with the feelings they have.

Time allows children to accept what has happened, to cope with the loss, and to avoid becoming involved in disputes. Time allows them to express their emotions, their anger and sadness, and to understand that they are not to blame.

Changes associated with family breakdown

There are many changes that children may have to face. Separation may bring **practical changes** like moving house, changing school, new friends, new routine, a different standard of living. It may mean losing touch with family and friends. The remaining parent may now work and the children may have new responsibilities at home.

Separation may bring **emotional changes** like feeling very sad, getting very angry, missing one parent, wanting to blame someone and experiencing a range of powerful emotions. It may involve anxiety about the future, anxiety about the departed parent and fear of being left by the remaining parent. It may mean coping with parents' emotions and behaviour, and experiencing divided loyalties.

Adults supporting children need to be careful not to make assumptions about their behaviour. For example, because they are playing happily does not mean that the pain has gone. Also, children will behave differently in different places. They may be fine with a parent at home but be very difficult in school. (They may be withdrawn with grandparents.) We must take care to allow children to show their different feelings – they do not have to be brave.

Children's reactions to separation and divorce

Up to 5 years
At this age children have limited understanding and are likely to escape into fantasy. Young children under stress are likely to bed-wet and/or have nightmares. They may show anxiety about meeting the other parent/partner. Their need is for brief but clear instructions, the maintenance of routines, extra comforters such as soft food and cuddles, and security objects.

Age up to 8 years
They may have worries about losing the rest of their family. They can become messenger between partners. If the children are with mum then girls may become the confidante of the mother. Their needs are for questions to be answered sensitively, encouragement to maintain childhood interests and brief but regular chats.

Age up to 12 years
With the onset of adolescence, children can become more reluctant to talk. They may feel embarrassed, especially as they often have strong ideas about right and wrong. They may launch into other activities to escape, such as school work. They need sensitive reminders of reality to normalise their feelings and reactions, and for their behavioural problems to be treated matter of factly.

It is a fact that boys and girls differ in how they respond to the family breakdown.

1. Boys seem more vulnerable because they hide their feelings and act in dramatic and negative ways which tend not to gain them sympathy or understanding. It is still usual for children to remain with their mothers, therefore boys lose their same sex parent and potential role model. Boys often take up role of being 'the man of the house', a role that can cause difficulties.
2. Girls seem to cope better because they express their feelings in a way that gains them understanding and sympathy. They are more likely to talk problems out rather than act them out.

In school the behaviour of children involved in family breakdown may change, their work standard may fall as they find it more difficult to concentrate or they fail to complete homework. They may be more prone to tears or outbursts of aggression towards authority figures. Such changes indicate how they are dealing with their home circumstances. Remember their behaviour is telling us something: behaviour *never* says nothing.

Understanding children's reactions can help us to respond to them in a more informed and caring way. Some of the reactions that may be observed are:

The withdrawn child

I cannot cope with what is happening. I am frightened and anxious about what else might happen. I feel I can't trust people and feel safer if I keep away from them, that way I can avoid being hurt and rejected again. *Message*: I need someone who will help me accept that it wasn't my fault, who can help me see my own strengths and qualities and will. It would help if I knew what is happening and what is likely to happen. I need to know my routine.

The angry child

I cannot face what is happening. I want to blame someone and make them make things right again. I will be angry in school especially to children who seem to have those very things that I want. *Message*: I need someone to help me accept my feelings and to release them in safer ways, perhaps painting or pottery. I need to be taught alternative ways to release my feelings. There will be times when I get so angry that I need to know what I can do and where I can go to until I calm down.

The parental child

I have to be strong and brave. This will allow me to be a helper for my mummy/ daddy. I will use all my emotional energy to show that I can cope. *Message*: I need someone to be in charge, to tell me what to do. I need times when I can relax and have fun and not feel responsible for everyone else.

The despairing child

I feel so alone and rejected. I understand the loss of my mum/dad and I am totally devastated by it. I long for them but I know that they have left. *Message*: I need someone who can accept my tears and my hurt by just making time to be with me. Someone who will give me ideas as to how I can cope from day to day. Someone who will remind me gently that while things are bad, I can cope.

The revengeful child

I feel so hurt by what has happened. At times I feel a strong urge to hurt other children or spoil their work. I have been hurt and I feel they should know what it is like as well. *Message*: I need to be allowed to show my feelings in safe ways. I need help to accept that what has happened was not done to hurt me. I need support to recognise my qualities and successes, and ideas to help me deal with these strong feelings. For instance, time out or special one-to-one time with people who care about me.

Boys and girls will often try to distance themselves from the disputes at home. They may seek shelter in friendships. Relationships can give support and some relief from the family conflicts as well as maintaining self-esteem. Often children can believe that they caused the break-up. Perhaps the final argument/fight was about something to do with them. So it is very important to help them understand that parents leave each other because of personal difficulties: they do not leave each other because of family difficulties. Figure 9.3 is a checklist for teachers who are supporting pupils involved in a family breakdown.

The Appendix Section 2 contains further notes on building concepts of loss into everyday teaching, and on parental information.

In school support
Does the pupil have the opportunity to talk with a
named member of staff?
Has the child a friendship group which could offer support?
Have the child's routines been maintained with little change?
Are you aware of the family's routine for picking the child up from school?
Do you meet with the parent regularly?
Do you have opportunities to hold meetings with other key support staff?

Being a good listener
Do you give child time to tell you his/her story?
Do you know what key emotions the child is experiencing?
Do you know which is the child's main 'grieving task'?
Have you given the child permission to show his/her feelings?

The Children Act
Are you familiar with the Children Act?
Do you have the addresses of the key adults involved with the pupil?
Do you supply information systematically to all who need to know?

Check the curriculum
Do you have books on divorce and separation in the library?
Do you teach information about 'modern families' rather than stereotypes?
Are you prepared for such special occasions as Mothers' Day and Fathers' Day?
Do children have opportunities to recognise and discuss changing family structures?

Monitoring
Is there a system for all involved to feed information to monitor a childs progress?
Do you have access to support to discuss any concerns you have?

Figure 9.3 A checklist for teachers supporting pupils involved in family breakdown

---

Key points

1. The painful reactions that children experience through loss are normal and understandable feelings.
2. Children's need for support will vary according to their age and understanding.
3. Children will experience similar emotions to adults but can lack coping strategies.
4. Maintaining contact with a child's carers will ensure that sensitive and effective support is offered.
5. Through including aspects of loss in the school curriculum, teachers can ensure that children are better placed to cope with the losses they will face.

10 Anxiety and Panic

Anxiety is a perfectly normal reaction to abnormal circumstances. Children, like adults, feel anxious when they perceive a threat is present. Their anxiety increases if they perceive that the threat presents real danger to them physically or emotionally or they are unable to deal with the threat adequately.

Adults encountering the anxious child are 'emotionally programmed' to comfort the child and simultaneously to seek to minimise the stressors which are at the root of the child's anxiety.

Some children are more prone to anxiety than others. Like any other mental health problem there are risk factors which increase or decrease the likelihood of coping or otherwise. Factors which increase the risk of mental health problems in young people according to NHS Advisory Service (1995) are: child risk factors, genetic influences, low IQ and learning disability, specific developmental delay, communication difficulty, difficult temperament, physical illness – especially chronic or neurological, academic failure, low self-esteem, family risk factors, overt parental conflict, family breakdown, inconsistent or unclear discipline, hostile and rejecting relationships, failure to adapt to child's changing developmental needs, abuse – physical/sexual and/or emotional, parental psychiatric illness, parental criminality, alcoholism and personality disorder, death and loss – including loss of friendships, environmental risk factors, socio-economic disadvantage, homelessness, disaster, discrimination, other significant life events.

Recognising anxiety problems in children

Making a judgment about whether a child is presenting anxiety problems is difficult because it involves social judgment. (Children may keep anxieties to themselves it is generally accepted that holding on to anxieties can become a problem). When teachers can perceive that a child has a problem with anxiety they will be reacting to the outward signs of anxiety.

Children who are anxious may:

- refuse to talk in specific situations;
- be reluctant to attend school;
- show excessive mood swings;
- have impaired relationships;
- tend to self abuse;
- suffer reduced concentration skills;
- exhibit increased inattentiveness and distractibility;
- show eating disorders (more so as adolescence approaches);
- misbehave;

- show physical symptoms such as nausea, palpitations, breathlessness, feeling dizzy or light-headed;
- develop obsessions or phobias;
- experience disturbed sleep patterns such as nightmares and can therefore often be tired in school.

When considering whether a child is presenting anxiety problems the teacher may move on a continuum of mild concern through to severe problems according to the following criteria detailed in DES Circular 1994: frequency; persistence; severity; abnormality; behaviour compared with normal expectation for a child of the age concerned.

A menu of anxiety problems

There are many anxieties which are either accepted or tolerated as being within the range.

Anxieties that are allowed are: physical threat, aggression, loud noises, heights, confined spaces, speed, explosions, wild animals, darkness, infectious disease, social exclusion.

Anxieties that are tolerated are: deadlines for work, the unknown, creepy crawlies, water, mice, looking foolish, being photographed, flying, domestic animals, lack of cleanliness, bacteria, silence, supernatural, cameras and disapproval from family and peers.

The following anxieties are more often regarded as a problem: cracks in the pavement, fruit, denim.

The list seems endless. Further complicating factors arise from the considerable differences in our acceptance of anxiety responses in the above 'tolerated' zone at different ages. The expectation for boys and girls can be different, as well as between children of different physical builds. If teachers encounter a tiny girl crying their reaction will be very different from when they encounter a large able boy displaying the same behaviour. Different emotions will be stirred in teachers as a result of these two contrasting experiences.

Flashbacks

Following a traumatic or abusive experience, children and adults can associate particular sensory experiences with the memory of that event. A noise, a smell, certain lighting conditions, a phrase, music and many everyday sensory experiences can become a trigger for a survivor of trauma. Yule (1991) indicates that 30–50 per cent of children will show a post-traumatic stress reaction and this can result in post-traumatic stress disorder (PTSD) in worst-case situations. Critical incident stress debriefing can help the child to understand the nature of flashbacks and to devise ways of coping. Focused discussion can also help the teacher to be more sensitive to the circumstances that may provoke strong feelings in a child. Once the situation is understood it is more likely that coping strategies can be developed (see Chapter 3).

There will be a gradual lessening of the impact of a post-traumatic stress reaction over time. It is also possible to treat PTSD, should that develop, using individual or group therapy. There can, however, be a residual effect which lives with the individual for a long period of time. The key influences are the severity of the initial trauma and the psychological strength of the individual.

Autistic spectrum disorder (Asperger Syndrome)

Anxiety is a well known feature of many disorders or disabilities. Autistic spectrum disorder (ASD) is the generic term covering a wide range of pervasive developmental disorders (Seach 1999, Wing 1996). The anxiety arises from a combination of difficulties referred to as the 'triad of impairment': social communication; social relationships; imagination.

Many children with ASD have associated learning difficulties and/or language difficulties. It is likely that adults will anticipate such children experiencing emotional difficulties. That does not make responding to them easier, because of their communication difficulties. Being unable to communicate basic needs can result in startling displays of frustration. A specialist teacher of children with ASD once responded to the question 'how do you deal with challenging behaviour?' by saying 'the first thing I ask is: what is this child trying to say to me?'

Although the difficulties of children with Asperger Syndrome are generally fewer than those with other forms of autism, their life can be complicated by the expectations placed upon them:

> Any social contact can generate anxiety as to how to start, maintain and end the activity and conversation. School becomes a social minefield; at any moment you can put a foot wrong. The natural changes in daily routine and expectation cause intense distress while certain sensory experiences can be unbearable (Attwood 1998).

Attwood (1998) suggests strategies to reduce anxiety for children with Asperger Syndrome:

- reassurance in specific situations (experience will reveal which circumstances or groups of children produce anxiety);
- use of a stress management programme (such as the panic management programme outlined below);
- catching the anxiety early by noting triggers and warning signs;
- relaxation;
- diversion to alternative activity (probably a familiar routine);
- use of focused physical exertion;
- avoiding stress-inducing situations;
- providing an alternative to school, such as focused home tuition;
- medication.

Responses to panic attacks

One particular manifestation of anxiety is the panic attack. This becomes a problem if there is a recurrent, unexpected pattern of an inability to cope with physical symptoms: The *Oxford English Dictionary* defines panic as 'a sudden and infectious fright leading to needless flight'.

The following programme is a cognitive behavioural based approach which has much in common with 'anger management' strategies. It is based upon the principle that an emotional response to a problematic situation provokes a fight or flight reaction in the individual. Given the close relationship between these two emotional reactions it should be possible to use the same cognitive approaches to managing both anger and panic problems.

Why use this approach? Panic is a response to an immediate crisis. It has important after-effects on the individual in the group. A reduced capacity to form meaningful relationships can leave the individual isolated and, therefore, more likely to experience the circumstances that provoke panic attacks. There is thus a vicious circle of increasingly inappropriate behaviour and vulnerability to panic attack.

Panic attacks represent a dysfunctional yet very powerful method for enabling an individual to control worrying situations. Any approach attempts to break into that vicious circle and enable individuals to control the problem and keep control of themselves. Panic attacks result in pupils:

- running away from challenging situations;
- experiencing difficulties in relating to the group, who perceive running away as a sign of weakness;
- being excluded from the peer group, leading to social isolation;
- losing coping skills, with the likelihood of feeling pressured again and again, without support of the group, resulting in a fight or flight decision.

Goals of a management programme

The goals are to moderate, to regulate and to provide appropriate expressions of response to the events which cause panic. The pupils need to explore each incident to find out which events are more likely to trigger panic attacks. They are then asked to explore the consequences of the course of action they chose to take. The following aspects are thus explored:

- thoughts (what did you *think* about when you were panicking?)
- feelings (what did you *feel* when you were panicking?)
- actions (what did you *do* when you were panicking?)
- outcomes (what are the *end results?)*

A management programme should aim to develop:

1. **Control**: to enable pupils to increase their ability to control feelings of panic and to increase the speed at which they can control those feelings.
2. **Confidence**: to enable pupils to feel confident that they can control their feelings.
3. **Respect**: to enable pupils to feel that they can be relied upon to control their feelings now and in the future.
4. **Integrity**: to move to a situation where the pupils control their response to their own feelings because of their responsibility to and for others.
5. **Assessment**: to increase pupils' ability to recognise the internal signs of panic and respond appropriately to them.
6. **Self-instruction**: to enable pupils to talk themselves through a panic attack.
7. **Problem solving**: to enable pupils to choose the most appropriate control skills.

Making use of imagery

Panic attacks are very frightening to the victims. They quickly become frightened of becoming frightened. One way of reducing the fear is to increase understanding of the process of panic, and that can be aided by the use of imagery. Lots of images could be chosen. For this example we shall use a washing machine with a special fast spin cycle. It is not part of the normal programme but is there for special cases where there is a need to make sure that the washing gets extra special treatment (a bit like panic being there for those times when we need that little bit of extra protection). Sometimes the washing machine may gets its programmes a bit muddled and set off the extra fast spin unnecessarily.

Example of use of imagery

Ask the child to imagine the washing machine going through its normal cycle. It does lots of different things, some slow, some fast and sometimes with rests in between. Talk about how the child's day may match different parts of the washing machine's cycle. Then talk about what happens when the extra fast spin is activated.

The trigger can be likened to the extra fast spin warning light coming on. As soon as that happens everything starts to move rapidly. Sometimes we will know who pressed that button to start the fast spin. Sometimes, however, we may not know how it came to be working. There follows a feeling of things running rapidly out of control whether or not we know who pressed the button. We very quickly move to a self-sustaining cycle: see Figure 10.1

Talk about how the components of the self-sustaining cycle feed off one another.

Discuss the component parts of the build-up to a panic attack.

Triggers result in mind reactions which lead to feelings of: frustration, annoyance, threat, irritation, hassle, anger, and fear.

These, in turn, result in bodily arousal reactions: facial expression, posture, muscle tension, feeling sick, butterflies, heart thumping, breathlessness, sweating, trembling, dry mouth, cold clammy hands, difficulties in concentration and wanting to go to the toilet.

From reactive to proactive mode

One of the features of panic attacks is that the 'response' behaviour is usually well established before the teacher gets the chance to do anything about it. Much of the initial work done in helping children to cope in the face of a panic attack will be reacting to events. It is important that some method is used to elicit from the pupil the elements of the situation as described earlier: thoughts, feelings, actions, and outcomes. These can be discussed with the pupil following each incident or can be written down on a record sheet and discussed with a member of staff later. By discussing these aspects systematically the teacher can build up a picture of:

● the circumstances which are likely to provoke panic attacks;
● what is happening from the pupil's perspective;

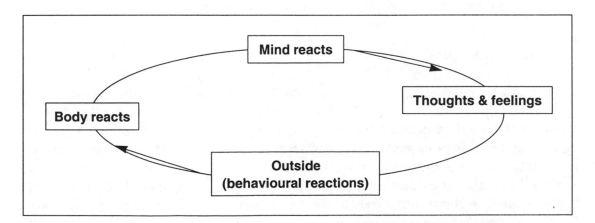

Figure 10.1 The self-sustaining cycle

- the differences between the pupil's perception of what happened and that of the teacher in charge at the time;
- possible indicators of strategies that can be used to help the pupil;
- the extent to which the pupil wants or has sufficient understanding to overcome the problem.

Increasingly the dialogue needs to focus on identifying strategies that will prepare the pupil for future difficulties. These points are worth remembering in discussions:

1. It is important for the adult to maintain a positive regard for the pupil. It is likely that any behaviour that has become a problem will be deep rooted and will take time to change.
2. It is likely that there will be setbacks particularly in the early stages. Maintaining a positive regard for the pupil in the face of setbacks can be very difficult to do. Ultimately, however, it will pay dividends.
3. It becomes easier to do the above if the adult adopts a strategy which is hard on issues but soft on the person.
4. The teacher must be vigilant in avoiding drifting into colluding with the pupil. Inevitably, as a close working relationship builds up with pupils it is possible to find their explanation of events more plausible and this can give rise to a distrust of colleagues.
5. Adults in discussion of problems should assertively challenge irrational/negative perceptions on the part of the pupil.

In the initial stages of a programme to help children cope with panic attacks, they may be offered an agreed place of sanctuary to withdraw to. This is a risky strategy because it could be seen to be rewarding inappropriate behaviour. It may, however, be preferable to set up an agreed sanctuary for a time-limited period rather than have the child running out of school.

If it is agreed that a sanctuary should be used it is important to establish clear ground rules for its usage first. These might be that the aim of the programme is for the pupil to be able to remain in all lessons on their timetable; that sanctuary arrangements are temporary whilst 'working towards' the appropriate classroom controls; that all members of staff are aware of any such arrangements.

Initial signs of success will therefore be a gradual reduction in the number of times that the sanctuary is used, and the length of time it is used. It is therefore vital that an appropriate method of recording is used to monitor the programme.

Like any individual behaviour programme it is important to record: when the plan was formulated; when it is to be implemented; how it is to be monitored; the success to be used in evaluation.

Strategies

Teachers can use a range of different strategies. To a certain extent the choice of appropriate programmes will be determined by what appears to have helped a pupil most in the past.

Breathing control

Place one hand on the stomach, take short calm breaths in through the nose and out through the mouth. The breathing should be relatively shallow but continuous (not panting). Repetition of a word like calm, relax, cool down can help to focus the mind on the process.

Deep breathing and backward counting
Take a deep breath in through the nose and as you breathe out through the mouth say 10. Repeat the exercise and say 9, moving slowly and calmly back to 0.

Deep breathing and pleasant thinking
Use the deep breathing technique but close the eyes, imagining a pleasant scene. Instead of counting, describe to yourself the smells, colours and sounds of that scene.

Reframing incidents which have gone wrong
Talk through the incident replacing key actions and stating what might have happened if the alternative action had been taken.

Thought stopping
Interrupt negative thoughts. Practise thinking negative thoughts then, when an adult says stop, switch to more positive thoughts. Pupils can practise using this skill in everyday situations and may eventually be able to offset panic attacks using this technique.

Talking sense to myself
Recognise the symptoms of a panic attack. As soon as pupils detect any of the danger signals they should talk themselves through the incident. For example, 'I'm going to be okay. There are people here to help me. I can cope with this situation in the same way that I have coped with situations like this before. I need to slow down my thinking, remain calm and let the teacher know that I am feeling anxious'.

Stop Think Do
Keep this useful adage in mind when facing challenging situations (it is also the title of a Social Skills Training Programme widely used in Australia and which is gradually being used in schools in the UK).

Developing an internal dialogue

The strategies described above encourage pupils to monitor their own responses to situations through internal dialogue. In this way they develop their meta-cognitive skills and become more adept, first at understanding their own responses, and second at adapting them as they are experiencing them. Pupils' internal dialogue should cover:

- reminders: of the danger times and the response they want to make;
- encouragement: that they will not be beaten by the problem, they do have the resources to overcome difficulties;
- questioning: 'What should I do now?' and 'What would be the best way to deal with this problem?'
- reassurance: referring back to previous problems that have been overcome;
- guidance: 'It will help me now if I deep breathe', or 'I should seek help from Miss Jones now';
- reward: recognising when a potentially difficult situation has been overcome and congratulating themselves.

Following up panic incidents

Each occasion when the pupil has to leave lessons should be recorded and followed up with a discussion between class teacher and child.

In a primary school this can be more problematic because of the close relationship between the class teacher and the pupils in her class. In a secondary school environment the pupil is moving from class to class and it is therefore easier for the form tutor to deal with incidents in a depersonalised way.

In the primary school setting there is greater potential for class teachers to feel that they have failed when a child has to leave their lesson because of a panic attack. It becomes more difficult for teachers to be objective when they are so close to a situation. In such cases it is probably better if the SENCO, head teacher or deputy does the follow-up discussion with the pupil. Maintaining trust between the class teacher and the teacher responsible for follow-up can be a challenge and will call upon each to practise extra vigilance in safeguarding professionalism.

The follow-up to a panic attack can take a variety of formats. In all cases the follow-up should offer the opportunity for undisturbed time to allow pupil and teacher to reflect on what has happened, and to consider ways of reframing the circumstances that allow for a more controlled response in the future. It will be important to record all incidents through a log kept by the teacher or the pupil self recording. The follow-up discussion should consider the following:

- When did the panic attack occur?
- Is any pattern of behaviour evident from this and previous incidents?
- What were the antecedents to the attack?
- What was the pupil thinking at the time when he/she left the lesson?
- What were the pupil's feelings when he/she left the lesson?
- What did the pupil do when he/she left the lesson?
- What has resulted from the pupil leaving the lesson?
- What other course of action could the pupil have taken? e.g.: asking for teacher's permission to change seats, writing down concerns to be discussed later, averting eye contact from a troublesome pupil.
- What would have been the possible result if the pupil had taken the other course of action (identified in previous question)?
- What can be done now to resolve the issues that brought about the panic attack?

Techniques for response control

Response control techniques are outlined in Figure 10.2 (Sheldon 1995). Interventions could range from a simple use of a particular approach as and when in the classroom to a very detailed intervention supervised by a clinician. The extent to which any approach is adopted will be determined by the persistence of the problem and the extent to which the problem interferes with the child's ability to cope with everyday life. Interventions should follow the principle of parsimony: small interventions should be used for small problems, with the complexity of the response only increasing relative to the complexity of the problem. Remembering this, and paying regard to the recommendations of the Code of Practice, a hierarchy of interventions could be considered as follows:

- class teacher working with child on a simple programme to reduce anxiety;
- class teacher working cooperatively;
- class teacher and SENCO;
- consultation with outside professionals;

Technique	Main Feature	Application
Modelling	Demonstration of key elements in behaviours likely to prove useful to client. Usually coupled with positive feedback on successive approximation from client.	Used for learning deficits of all kinds plus vicarious extinction of fears and phobias.
Social Skill Training	As above, but with extra emphasis on rehearsing social and conversational skills and deciding on which occasions a given performance is appropriate.	Used for withdrawn and unconfident clients; people with learning disabilities; psychiatric patients; children; and in work with delinquents where such deficits can be implicated in offending.
Assertion Training	As 'modelling' above, but with extra emphasis on fears associated with assertiveness, and on discriminating between assertive and aggressive responses.	Used with excessively shy or withdrawn individuals. Often used in groups and as an adjunct to wide programmes.
Self Management Techniques	Designed to teach coping skills. Emphasis on helping clients to develop techniques to re-label their experiences and change expectations of personal efficacy and the likely outcome of their behaviours. Also teaches clients to obtain environmental support for new responses by changing contingencies.	Used in a wide range of personal problems, especially with deficits and avoidance behaviours resulting from these.
Cognitive Approaches	Means of identifying the personal constructs applied to self and to problems and making appropriate changes in these.Emphasis on use of positive self-statements and self-reinforcement to maintain new responses.	Useful for wide range of performance difficulties. Particularly applicable to relatively unstructured field settings. Can be used in conjunction with other behavioural programmes.
Positive Counter Conditioning	The introduction of a response capable of inhibiting anxiety to weaken conditioned anxiety reactions.	Used in the treatment of specific fears and anxieties.
Exposure Therapy (de-sensitising)	Controlled but rapid exposure to threatening stimuli maintained until anxiety extinguished.	Can be used to control excessive fears, panic attacks and phobias in co-operative clients

Slow Exposure	Gradual exposure to hierarchy of threatening stimuli, initially to the accompaniment of muscular relaxation (systematic desensitisation).	Used to control excessive fears and phobias where clients are unable to co-operate with rapid exposure. (Muscular relaxation component can be used independently to overcome stress reactions.)
Bio-feedback	Use of electronic instruments to amplify and display data from bodily processes such as heart rate, galvanic skin response and blood pressure, with a view to bringing these under conscious control.	The introduction of a response capable of inhibiting anxiety to weaken conditioned anxiety reactions.

Figure 10.2 Summary of Response Control techniques used by therapists

- referral to a service external to the school, e.g. Educational Psychology Service on Child and Adolescent Mental Health Services;
- clinical referral.

Responding to pupils who panic: developing teacher's skills

The following activities can be used at staff meetings or on training days to help develop the skills of teachers and classroom support assistants in responding to children who experience panic attacks. As they develop a range of skills all staff members will be able to deal more confidently and therefore more calmly in the face of a child panicking.

1. In small groups complete a strengths and weaknesses chart showing how your school works effectively with anxious children.
2. The following activity could be helpful in a staff meeting or in a parents' group meeting when drawing up school policies or procedures.
   a. Working in pairs describe to each other a time when you were very anxious and worried. Describe your thoughts, feelings, actions, what you did, and finally what you wish you had done.
   b. Discuss how that situation might have worked out differently if you had reacted in the way you wished you had.
   c. Feed back to the wider group what you have learnt about the way your school should respond to anxious children.
3. Try to identify features of your own teaching practice where you have successfully used an approach which matches one of the following approaches: modelling; social skill training; assertiveness; teaching coping skills; desensitising.
4. Role play: Act out a scene in which a child panics and the teacher attempts to calm the child down. In group discussion afterwards reflect on the tone of voice used by the teacher, the posture and the feelings, what worked well and what didn't work quite so well.
5. Discussion with Educational Psychologist/Occupational Therapist/Speech and Language Therapist.
6. Hold regular case discussions within the staff team to generate good practice through peer support/supervision.

Key points

1. Anxiety is a normal reaction to abnormal circumstances.
2. Some children are more prone to anxiety than others.
3. A wide range of factors increase the risk of children and young people suffering anxiety related difficulties.
4. Indicators for assessing the presence of anxiety related problems are the frequency, persistence, severity or abnormality of associated behaviour compared with normal expectation for a child in the same age group.
5. Particular sensory experiences may vividly recall the memory of a traumatic experience. These are called flashbacks and can be a source of considerable anxiety.
6. Anxiety is a feature of autistic spectrum disorder (ASD) resulting from difficulties in social communication, social relationships and imagination.
7. Panic attacks are an extreme reaction to anxiety.
8. A range of techniques can be used to teach children strategies to anticipate and cope with panic.

11 Anger Management

Anger is a normal healthy emotion and can be a response to the loss of loved ones or cherished objects. It is also a key emotion for survival: it energises us for fight or flight when we are threatened. As an emotion anger can be expressed positively or negatively. In school we are naturally concerned with its negative expression through verbal and aggressive behaviour. How can we support children who seem to be trapped by their anger? Their anger is making their lives and the lives of others unhappy.

The dynamics of anger

Anger demands attention and can lead to aggressive or depressive behaviour. It is a panic response, indicating that those who become angry believe themselves, rightly or wrongly, to be in danger. Once anger becomes a dominating emotional response it will lead children to behave in ways that self perpetuate it. Anger needs to be recharged. The way anger is released is typically through aggressive behaviour which leads to people rejecting the angry person or behaving aggressively in return. Both of these responses will cause more anger, creating a vicious circle.

Understanding anger

The more we understand anger the better able we will be to manage it. In school aggressive children usually learn less and disrupt lessons. They often hurt others and while they may seem confident they usually have a low self-esteem.

There are many reasons why some children seem to be angrier than others. Clearly there will be temperamental and inherited differences. Anger can also be caused by aggressive role models and by learning that aggressive behaviour pays off. Children with learning difficulties may also experience frustration and become aggressive.

Note that anger can also be a response to abuse – physical, sexual or emotional. If you ever suspect this you must discuss your concerns with your school's child protection officer. Be careful not to either over-react or do nothing.

Anger in the classroom

While you will have little control over the exact size of your classroom there are other aspects you do have control over. To design a non-aggressive learning environment it might be helpful if we first consider what makes for an aggressive one, a class where we would expect conflict to happen often. We don't need to go into too much detail to make the point. Such a class would be ruled with hostility and criticism, with few rewards. Bare walls would show no value for work and litter/graffiti would be left to indicate that this is not a cared for place. Children would only be valued for their achievements, which would encourage competition, and place no value on effort. The more angry a person is then the more this will be reflected in their outside world.

Because our physical world gives rise to internal emotional reactions we need to capitalise on this to ensure that, though small, we use our space positively. Some ideas for creating a positive and non-aggressive learning environment are shown in Figure 11.1.

Classroom management

Rules

Angry children will often push the boundaries and test the rules. These children need boundaries all the more; without them they would have even more difficulties. Therefore set clear, positive rules and make it clear that these rules are extremely important and will be enforced. Children trying to cope with extreme anger need the security of knowing what the rules are. Rules show that you care enough to protect them from negative behaviour.

The core of positive classroom rules is respect for others, self and property; but you should involve the children in formulating both the rules and the consequences for following them or not. You will probably have to temper their sanctions with the 'milk of adult kindness'. Make sure that all children in your class feel safe, belong, have choices, feel free and have fun.

**Ideas for a Positive
Physical Environment**

Lively displays – not just wall papering!
Plants – empathy with nature
Equipment that is organised and clearly labelled
Books, books and more books
Private space
Resources made available to children
Positive messages, e.g. 'Thank You for Walking'
A place to recognise achievements, celebrating
Reflective quiet area
Stimulation outside the normal
for example natural sounds – whales and dolphins
mood music
Powerful evocative words such as CARE, TOGETHER, SUCCESS colourfully displayed
Inspirational sayings and funny cartoons

Figure 11.1 Creating a non-aggressive learning environment

The anger mountain

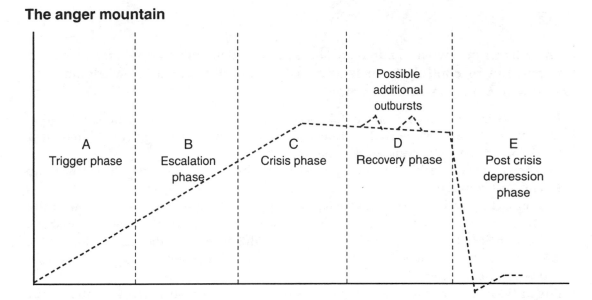

Figure 11.3 The anger mountain

The phases of anger are shown in Figure 11.3. How quickly any child enters any phase will vary between individuals. This model gives insight into the process of anger with indications as to where interventions can be made. It is clear that once a child is into the Crisis phase there is little chance of a rational solution. At that point an adult is concerned with 'damage limitation'. What is happening here is that an emotional solution is being sought for a problem, this is a biological flight or fight response. Children are telling us that they are unable to cope with the demands of the situation and have been pushed to respond with a panic response.

Using the Anger Mountain idea we can develop a useful aide-mémoire which can help us to check our responses at the various stages, Before, During and After. Having some plan of action that you are working from will give you a sense of control. It is important to keep referring back to your plan. You will often not respond as you wanted to, that is natural. But having a plan can help you see areas where your responses are helping and those areas that you wish to develop.

Before

1. **Remain calm** To let children's anger hurt you is to give them power over you. Avoid power struggles with children. Leave them a way out; cornered children are more likely to quickly go up the 'anger mountain'.
2. **Acknowledge their feelings** Denying anger, or trivialising it, fuels anger. 'I can see you're very annoyed' is much better than 'Come on there's no need to feel like that'.
3. **Use solution type questions** It can help children to remind them that they have successfully dealt with situations like this before. 'Can you remember what helped last time?'
4. **Time out** Having a quiet corner in the room where a child can go to for a few minutes can enable children to collect their thoughts and calm down.
5. **Attention diverters** Have ready a set of activities that can be quickly used to divert a child's attention into a very different activity.
6. **Active relaxation** Make sure you have trained children to carry out several relaxation techniques such as deep breathing, counting back from 10.
7. **Tension releasers** Physical activity can help children release their anger. Any activity that involves their hands will be especially good, e.g. modelling in clay or tearing paper for a 'bean bag'. (Current research suggests that excessive activity, punching pillows, shouting out the anger, can leave children even angrier.)

During

There will be times when children are at the peak of their anger mountain and are in a rage and out of control. At such times asking questions or acknowledging their feelings will not be possible or appropriate.

1. **Posture** Keep your hands visible, unfolded and palms visible. This avoids the child fearing what cannot be seen and is a non-threatening position. Avoid towering over children; sit or bend down to be on the same level as the child.
2. **Proximity** Avoid entering the child's personal space by keeping a reasonable distance – up to a metre – between you.
3. **Eye contact** Excessive eye contact can be challenging and confrontational. Allow the child to look away or avoid eye contact. The 'look at me when I am talking' will escalate matters.
4. **Voice tone** Speak calmly but firmly. Make it clear what you expect the child to do. Use the 'broken record' technique: 'I can see that you are angry, but I want you to go to the corner and wait for me to come.'
5. **Fire drill** Make sure that all of your children know how to behave in 'crisis situations'. For example, a named child will go to the head teacher's office for assistance. All children will leave the room in an orderly fashion and assemble at an agreed place. Practice these as you would a normal Fire Drill.

After

1. **Check 'fire drill'** Did your crisis situation drill work as well as could be expected? If not, make changes and practise it more.
2. **Return to normal** Aim to show the child that you expect relationships to be back to normal; that no grudges are borne. It was the behaviour that was the concern not the child.
3. **Learning** When matters are calm discuss with the child what went wrong and look for skills that need to be practised more.
4. **Solution focused** Try to find slight signs of improvement. Was the 'rage' as long as usual? How long since the last one? Aim to find ways of showing the child that slowly matters are improving.
5. **Pay back** If another child has been hurt or upset it might help if the involved child tried to compensate for this; helping them; doing a painting for them; writing a story for them.
6. **Look for patterns** If there seems to be a pattern to when the child explodes with anger, look to any triggers that may be causing them to lose control. Is it during free time? Also, what happens after the explosion? Do they get a lot more attention? If there are any patterns then change what happens before and what follows such incidents.
7. **Improve relationships** If the same children seem to be involved then make time to improve the relationships between them. Set them tasks that require them to cooperate and then reward them for achieving a mutually shared goal.

Anger styles

The way in which we have talked about angry children so far is too general to be useful. We frequently talk as if children were similar in what makes them angry and how they express it. This is clearly not the case. Not all children 'act out' their anger. Schmidt (1993) has proposed a helpful way of categorising how children express their anger. With a better way of classifying 'anger' we will be able to design intervention much more precisely. It is also useful to think of anger as being capable of attacking others – 'acting out'; or if this is not safe to do, then 'acting in', attacking themselves.

Children who act in

Stuffers

Some children hold in their anger or even deny to themselves that they are angry. They will try to avoid confrontations at all costs. There are many reasons for an apparent fear of anger. Perhaps they fear the consequences of showing anger towards someone they love; or they cannot face accepting the pain or loss that the anger is in response to. As a result of bottling up their anger, these children tend to be prone to somatic illnesses and depression.

Withdrawers

Withdrawers will often express their anger by withdrawing from others. They will not mix with other children, trying to manage their anger through cutting themselves off. It is as if they are trying to protect themselves from the cause of their anger while punishing those they believe to have caused it.

Children who act out

Blamers

Children who tease, name-call and the like are often children who blame others for their angry feelings. They are externally controlled and blame others for any failure or negative feelings that they have. They have little belief in being able to make things better for themselves.

Exploders

These children express their anger through direct and immediate confrontation. They are often described as having 'short fuses' and being physically or verbally aggressive towards peers and or adults. They manage their feelings of anger through acting them out.

Children who think it out

Problem solvers

These children have qualities of patience and perseverance in managing their anger. They are open and accepting of other people's feelings and explore ways in themselves to better manage their anger.

Most of us at some time may have used one or more of these ways. The children we are concerned about seem to get stuck with one or two ways of managing their anger. The more we can understand their way of coping the better we will able to help them. These children have found a solution as to how they manage their anger. It is often not however the best. It has negative repercussions for both themselves and others. We need to show and/or teach them alternative ways. Like all other children these children want to belong, to be accepted and to be valued.

Anger management strategies

The core principle is that anger management is a compilation of stress reduction techniques for channelling one's angry feelings into socially acceptable directions. An anger management programme will therefore be a combination of relaxation techniques and specific interventions. The relaxation techniques given in the previous chapter under Responses to panic attacks – Strategies may be useful here.

Managing Anger

ACT IN

Stuffers and withdrawers

1. Have the children list those situations they find difficult to manage. Explore ways in which they could behave in these situations and help them practise the new skills.
2. Help the children learn those cues that they have for different emotions, physical, face, body and behaviour.
3. Explore safe ways such as art, drama, and music as ways of experiencing anger in a safe context.
4 Teach children 'coping self talk'. That is, positive statements to say, 'Breathe slowly, I can cope.'

5. Keep a journal of the children's progress through situations that they find difficult. Encourage them to write or draw their feelings.
6. Guided imagery: Ask the children to imagine a difficult situation, or a time when they felt angry. Talk them through their anger. Show them that being angry is a natural response to many situations.
7. Use stories, poetry, plays, films, etc with examples of children who overcame their personal difficulties rather than gave in to them.
8. Develop a 'daily record' for children to tick all their 'okay' feelings.

ACT OUT

Blamers

1. Provide regular contact with an adult who is calm, rational and consistent and does not respond negatively to their behaviour to review the children's progress.
2. Design a plan with children for alternative ways in which to behave when with peers. Explain behaviour that is expected and agree positive and negative outcomes for success.
3. Bin the sin. When children hurt others, have set activities for them to make up to the hurt child.

ACT OUT

Exploders

1. Always focus any reprimand on the children's behaviour.
2. Praise and reinforce examples of appropriate behaviour.
3. Involve the children in setting up a plan to reduce specific examples of problem behaviour with agreed outcomes.
4. Find an area of strength and utilise it in class and with other pupils.
5. Have an agreed 'bolt hole' for when – ever the children feel that they are beginning to become wound up.

Figure 11.4 Strategies for the management of different anger styles

Specific interventions

Figure 11.4 gives a range of strategies. Some may already be familiar to you. No 'quick fix' solution exists, but developing a plan of action is always a step in the right direction. It is important to make a point of supporting the child's self-esteem. It takes confidence to learn new skills. It is worth remembering that confrontations are rare where pupils and teachers enjoy good relationships.

Key points

1. Anger can be a healthy emotional response to a range of situations.
2. While aggressive behaviour needs to be firmly addressed, children can be supported to take control of their anger.
3. Confronting aggressive children involves learning skills to decrease their level of arousal.
4. Through studying aggressive behaviour we can learn to prevent it better, manage it better or learn from it.
5. Managing anger involves learning specific skills and relaxation techniques.

12 Epilogue: Teachers and School Morale

'Morale is a concept that is greatly discussed, little understood and difficult to define'
(Magoon and Linkous 1979).

This book has been about helping to understand children's emotions and the impact that emotional difficulties may have on a child in school. The effectiveness of teachers in recognising their pupils' emotional needs can depend on a wide range of personal and institutional factors. The aim of all schools must be to ensure that the teachers are able to respond competently and creatively to the needs of their pupils. Whether they are equipped to do this will in part depend on the support teachers provide for one another professionally and emotionally. One barometer of this support process is the morale of the team. Those schools that set out to improve the emotional well-being of the pupils could usefully examine how teams of teachers or the school organisation convey that teachers are valued. This could be a very useful starting point in the process of examining the emotional climate of the school.

The concept of morale

School inspection reports often make oblique or direct reference to the morale of the staff team, citing low morale as a cause of poor performance within a school. Yet morale has traditionally been poorly researched because of the difficulty in providing an adequate description of the concept. Wolman (1973) gives the following definition: 'Morale is an elusive quality that describes a person's satisfaction with membership in the organisation'.

It is a problematic term because of the 'they would say that, wouldn't they' factor. This is the outcome of the process that occurs when inspectors conclude that a school is failing. It's because of low morale on the staff team, say the teachers. It's because the teachers are poor in quality and unwilling to develop their skills, say the managers. Such polemics are developed in a culture of blame that has characterised the worst excesses of the recent era.

Despite problems of definition morale is used extensively as an indicator of organisational well-being or otherwise. Newspapers often use the term morale in stories about the impact on teachers of external forces such as curriculum changes and increased workloads. Government documents make reference to teachers' morale, as the Interim Advisor Committee on Teacher Pay and Conditions 1988 (DES 1994). The Elton Report (DES 1989) referred to the interrelation of teacher morale and good discipline in schools.

Teachers' morale is seen as reflected in the emotional commitment they make to their pupils and the profession. Morale is also related to the public image, status and behaviour of teachers and schools. High morale is associated with teacher confidence. Low morale seems to be clearly recognisable in behavioural outcomes.

Morale is clearly a very powerful concept describing strong feelings. Blum and Naylor (1968) described morale arising from four determinants:

- feelings of group solidarity;
- the need for a goal;
- observable progress towards that goal;
- individual participation in meaningful tasks necessary to achieve that goal.

In the seventies and eighties, Frederick Herzberg contributed a great deal to the understanding of the concept of morale which he used synonymously with the term 'job attitude'. He introduced the two-factor theory of job attitudes, which has formed the basis of a great deal of current thinking in personnel management. The two factors refer to the sources of employee attitudes:

1. **Hygiene factors** These are associated with the animal instinct for the avoidance of pain. Thus physical factors of the work environment as well as pay, recreation time and so on, need attention in order to maintain a contented work group.
2. **Motivational factors** These are based upon a fundamental need for humans to recognise achievement and to take responsibility.

The determinants of employee attitudes are a complex interaction between the above two factors.

> Job attitudes are a powerful force and are functionally related to the productivity, stability and adjustment of the industrial workforce. The difference between satisfiers and dissatisfiers… involves not only a qualitative difference in factors but a difference largely qualitative in effects. Specifically the positive effects of high attitudes are more important than the negative effects of low attitudes (Herzberg 1968).

Morale and team performance

Belbin (1981) looked at the effectiveness of occupational teams and why they succeed or fail. He saw morale as only a marginal factor. He concluded that poor morale usually revealed itself as a consequence of failure but that, in simulation exercises, some teams described as happy when they started out ended up with abysmal results.

> Even at the end (of the business management simulation exercise) members sometimes commented on how much they enjoyed working with one another. They went down smiling. Similarly intense personal conflicts often arose in a number of companies but that did not presage failure (Belbin 1981).

This leads to one principle of staff morale: morale in any task-focused team is related as much to the attainment of group goals as it is to friendship patterns within the group.

Belbin indicated the importance, in the long run, of the perceived success of the group in maintaining morale. He described the styles of contribution of various members of a working team and indicated that the most effective teams were not necessarily made up of similar types, although it always helps if team members are compatible. He identified the types within any team (see Figure 12.1).

Morale is strongly related to personal or team performance and the maintenance of positive feelings. It is clear from Belbin's work that leadership plays a significant role in this process but it is not the only constituent of effective teams. Indeed leadership can be as problematic a term as morale itself. It is difficult to describe in behavioural

Type	Personal qualities	Team Contribution	Allowable weaknesses
Plant	Creative, imaginative, unorthodox.	A solver of difficult problems.	Ignores detail. Too preoccupied to communicate effectively.
Resource Investigator	Extrovert, enthusiastic, communicative.	Explores opportunities. Develops contacts.	Overoptimistic Loses enthusiasm once the initial interest has passed.
Shaper	Challenging, dynamic. Thrives on pressure.	Has the drive and courage to overcome obstacles.	Proneness to provocation, irritation and impatience. Can hurt others, feelings.
Team-Worker	Cooperative, mild, perceptive and diplomatic.	Listens, builds, averts friction and calms the waters.	Indecisive in crunch situations. Can be easily influenced.
Co-ordinator	Mature, confident, a good chairperson.	Clarifies goals, promotes decision-making. Delegates well.	Can be seen as manipulative. Delegates personal work.
Specialist	Single-minded, self-sharing, dedicated.	Provides knowledge and skills in rare supply.	Contributes on only a narrow front. Dwells on technicalities. Overlooks the big picture.
Monitor Evaluator	Sober, strategic and discerning.	Sees all options. Judges accurately.	Lacks drive and ability to inspire others. Overly critical.
Implementer	Disciplined, reliable, conservative and efficient.	Turns ideas into practical actions.	Somewhat inflexible. Slow to respond to new possibilities.
Completer	Painstaking, conscientious, anxious.	Searches out errors and omissions and delivers on time.	Inclined to worry unduly. Reluctant to delegate. Can be a nit-picker.

Figure 12.1 The types within a team
(Adapted from Belbin RM (1993) *Team Roles at Work* Butterworth Heinemann.)

terms and, in making judgements about a leader's ability to lead, we are often making judgements about a group's willingness or ability to be led. Like morale, the term leadership is a judgement based on the outcomes of a given situation rather than clearly identified processes. The process of leadership involves many features: not least is a modicum of good luck.

Hunshelwood (1987) explored the impact of morale on workers in therapeutic establishments and the effect it has on their ability to cope with challenging situations. He looked at community and individual factors that contribute to overall morale. High morale was reflected in the ability of groups to discuss or handle difficult situations. Any change in the composition of the staff group is therefore likely to have a significant impact on morale. Of course, the more significant an individual is within the social network of the workplace, the greater the impact will be on morale if they are taken from the team.

Within any occupational group, their perceived level of success affects morale but that is only effective, according to Hunshelwood: 'When it is sustained on the basis of a cruelly accurate appreciation of reality'.

That reality is sustained more clearly when there is a recognisable output, as in a factory. Production figures can be used to confirm or contradict speculation about the performance of a team. It follows then that morale cannot be improved in isolation. Improvements in morale must be part of a group active learning cycle which includes achieving organisational goals (see Figure 12.2).

Factors likely to have a negative effect on morale are:

- misperceptions about the manageability of the task;
- conflict between goals;
- insufficient resources;
- poor relationships between colleagues;
- rivalry;
- lack of role clarity;
- where there is belittling criticism;
- where staff feel unsupported and unlistened to;
- where job hatred develops;
- where there is a lack of clear leadership.

This brings us to another important principle about morale: one central problem of low morale is that the outcomes of low morale have the effect of reducing morale.

Hunshelwood proposes a more elaborate model of morale than the active learning cycle (see Figure 12.3).

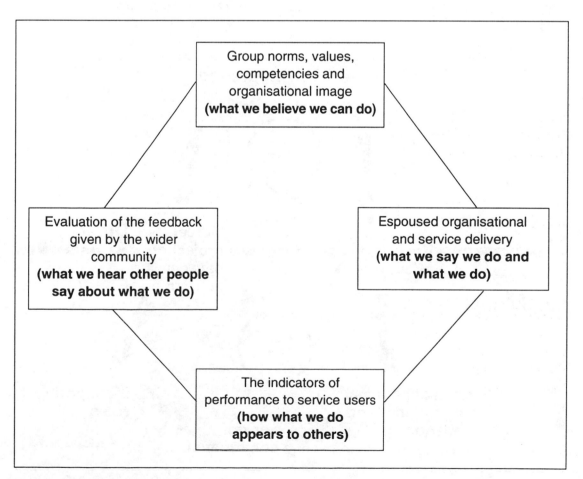

Figure 12.2 The group active learning cycle

The organisational outcomes of low morale can be:

- the creation of personal empires;
- cliques developing;
- disengagement from the group goals;
- confidence to move on falters.

The consequence of this process, if left unchecked, is demoralisation or the development of 'organisational learning disability' (Senge 1990), which is a self-sustaining malaise.

The literature on teacher morale is sparse and in the main refers to the impact of different aspects of the task, or context of teaching, on teachers' morale. Smith (1966, 1976) describe the features which contribute to high morale based on five distinct dimensions:

1. Group cohesion: teachers' cooperation and feelings of unity behind common school goals.
2. Tenacity and fortitude: the ability to endure frustration in overcoming difficulties.
3. Leadership synergy: representing the group energy generated and released by the school leaders.
4. Adventurous striving: enthusiasm and confidence in zealous striving to attain the school's goals.
5. Personal reward: incentives of personal satisfaction in the school situation.

All of the above relate in the main to the internal features of the staff team. The impact of external perceptions on morale is not, however, included here. Coverdale (1973) suggests that external perception of teaching through the media and government statements can have a significant impact on teacher morale. The ability of any staff team to weather external storms will relate to the framework of support within the staff team.

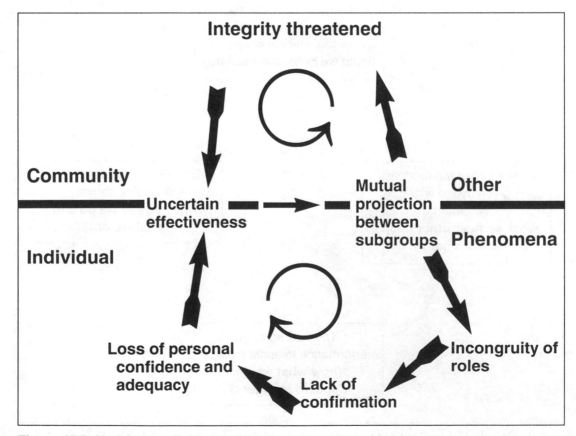

Figure 12.3 Hunshelwood's Model of the Dynamics of Low Morale

Fogell (1994) studied morale in six primary schools. His findings are summarised in the following questions and responses:

Does the concept of morale help in understanding the ways schools function?
- Teachers believed that a team with a high morale offered better teaching to the pupils than low morale teams.
- High morale was seen as a clear contributory factor to effective teaching.
- The term morale refers to feelings that can be decisive in the effectiveness of the team.
- Morale is multi-faceted and dynamic.
- The dynamic nature of morale also indicates that, when tackling ineffective schools, labelling schools can have a damaging effect on morale which, in turn, makes improvement more difficult to achieve.

How do schools identify high and low morale?
- Schools with high morale are seen to be team orientated, open and trusting, with high expectations and standards for all members of the community, and which care enough to present a pleasant place to work in.
- Schools with low morale are seen to be those where there is staffroom division. If divide and rule is countenanced as a short term control mechanism it may do little for the long term effectiveness of the staff team.
- Cliques were seen to be the strongest enemy of high morale. Low morale is epitomised by poor communication, disagreement about organisational goals, poor adherence to agreed objectives, and low commitment to the task of teaching.

In high morale schools the most common model of decision making seemed to be that of Grove (see Figure 12.4).

Is there any consistency in the understanding of the term morale?
- The evidence indicated a high degree of consistency of seeing morale as related to four dynamics in schools: interpersonal relationships, communication, goal focus and personal satisfaction.
- Morale in any school is determined by a complex interrelationship of internal and external factors.
- The level of agreement between head teachers, teachers and learning support staff in schools was high in relation to:
  (a) the indicators of high and low morale
  (b) internal factors that caused high and low morale
  (c) the current external issues in the school affecting morale.
- External factors affecting morale were identified as school inspections, legislative changes, government attitude towards education and teacher workload.

Do class teachers and head teachers view morale differently?
- Differences emerged between the groups in two ways. Teachers saw the behaviour of their colleagues as less likely to affect morale than did the head teachers and deputies. Head teachers considered morale to be critical in their leadership but were mindful of their limitations in controlling it.
- Morale was considered it to be less of an issue when things were running well.

How do schools respond to morale issues?
- In high morale schools the high level of communication and involvement in the decision-making process seemed to keep tensions under control.
- Schools dealt with maintaining high morale differently from dealing with low morale.
  (a) Maintaining high morale was seen to be a product of the levels of openness, involvement and responsibility within the organisation. It was clear that the maintenance of high professional standards was very important in this process.

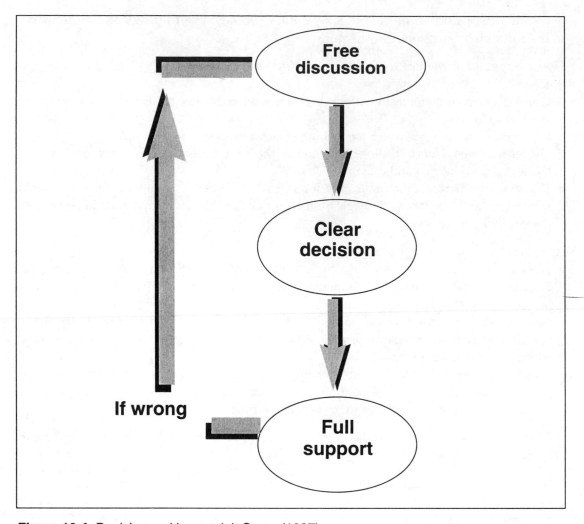

Figure 12.4 Decision making model, Grove (1987)

    (b) Low morale was dealt with by individualising the problem, providing support and easing the burden.
- Successful management of teacher morale is through organisations which are: 'hard on issues but soft on people'.

What practical approaches to improving morale are used by schools?
- A focus on high standards within the organisation.
- Lots of praise, recognition and thanks for good work (clearly such praise needs to be seen to be appropriate and that presents a problem for the leader).
- High levels of communication and openness.
- High levels of involvement in decision making.
- Flexibility in responding to the individual needs of teachers. One head teacher summed up the dilemma thus: 'You have to know the difference between maintaining high expectations and putting people under unacceptable pressure'. The mechanism for distinguishing the difference between these two was openness between all members of the organisation.

What is the relationship between written policies and morale?
- Whilst there were references to the care of all members of the community there were no reference to morale in any of the written policies of the schools.
- All of the schools had clear policies, which had been worked out by the above decision-making process
- Staff felt that they could change policies if they needed.

- The impact of such levels of agreement was clear. The outcomes of policy statements could be seen in the daily working of the schools.
- Strong school policies appeared to help schools cope better with externally imposed innovations. The staff felt confident that within their framework they could address external requirements, but at their pace.
- A general policy of continual reappraisal of policy and practice was evident in all schools but all stated that they filtered and paced external initiative so those teachers didn't become swamped.

The research supported the view that staff teams with a high morale have a greater potential to feel on top of their task and to offer a good service. Morale is a term that holds meaning for most people. It is a concept that will be used by those who make judgements about an organisation whether from within or without the school. It is therefore helpful that more is understood about the dynamics of morale.

By discussing issues of staff morale, the questions raised will bring all those who have responsibility for schools – pupils, parents, teachers, head teachers, inspectors, administrators, governors, and politicians – closer to understanding the complexities of the phenomenon, and the processes which are likely to effect change where there are problems. Or more importantly, avoid problems altogether.

Suggestions for improving morale within a teaching team

The following exercise can help to focus on issues of organisational morale and contribute towards an ethos of openness within the staff team.

1. Individually or in small groups complete Strengths Weaknesses Opportunities and Threats (SWOT) analyses of your school to compare views of the organisation and the issues it faces. Draw up a priority list of the things identified that you may wish to build upon, eliminate, do more of, do less of etc.
2. Discuss and agree new ground rules for staff meetings.
3. Introduce mentoring of newly appointed with more experienced teachers.
4. Analyse the teaching team using the Belbin descriptors. Discuss your findings (full details of the Belbin Questionnaires to assess team roles can be obtained by consulting the Belbin reference).
5. Divide up into quality circles and provide feedback to each other on the following questions:
   How can relationships be improved in our school?
   How can openness and communication be enhanced in our school?
   How can goal specification and adherence be improved in our school?
   How can our school make itself more pleasant to work in?
   How can leadership be enhanced in this school? What can the management team do to improve leadership? What can teachers do to make the job of leading easier?
   How can the external image of our school be improved?
   How can the external pressures on our school be accommodated?
6. Use a Process Consult (psychologist, adviser, management consultant) to offer reflections on the communications systems and processes within the school. Aubrey (1988) sums up the process: 'Process consultation focuses on groups and systems with the goal of a planned effort at the school self study and improvement, based on examination of formal and informal norms, structures and procedures, and interpersonal transactions that affect people's work and productivity and morale'.
7. Devise agreed response for emergencies or other serious circumstances in the staff team: illness, accident, harassment, family breakdown, bereavement.

Key points

1. Morale is strongly related to personal or team performance and the maintenance of positive feelings. It is less strongly related to friendship patterns within the group.
2. Schools can maintain morale by encouraging openness about the experience of working in a particular work group.
3. The central problem of low morale is that the outcomes of low morale have the effect of reducing morale.
4. There is often a mismatch between the levels of agreement evident in: a) describing a group of teachers as having low morale, and b) deciding on the most appropriate ways to tackle the difficulty.
5. Successful management of teacher morale is through organisations that are 'hard on issues but soft on people'.

Appendix

Section 1: Further notes on building self-esteem

General ideas

1. Develop your relationship with the pupils through:
   (a) listening to them
   (b) spending time together
   (c) encouraging their efforts and praising their successes.
2. Establish in children a sense of personal identity: what are their likes/dislikes in food, music, TV, books etc. Help them to see their uniqueness and their 'right to be who they are'.
3. Review the child's life, key events and key people. Produce a Family History Life Line with happy events.
4. Look for genuine achievements to praise, set meaningful goals. Make them Small, Specific, Achievable, Realistic and Timed over a set period (SMART).
5. Detail children's strengths and interests and utilise them in class/group projects.
6. Discuss with children a target they would like to achieve, consider with them appropriate strategies and support them in working out an Action Plan – step by step to ensure success.
7. Encourage children to join only those clubs and activities where they have the necessary skills.
8. Give frequent informal chats to listen to children's progress and boost their efforts.
9. Design a contract with them for new goals/behaviours with agreed awards. If new skills are needed make sure these are overlearned in a safe atmosphere before being tried out for real.
10. Give appropriate responsibilities and/or tasks. Ensure that these are both valued and meaningful.
11. Provide an older 'buddy' to support children through looking out for them, having a chat with them.
12. Ask children to help another child in areas where they have strengths.
13. Promote positive thinking. Get children to list their positive aspects of themselves.
    One thing I like about myself is
    . . . .
    My successes include
    . . . .
    My friends like me because
    . . . .
14. Set homework on small personal goals. I will
    . . . .
15. Work together on situations that cause anxiety and worry. Develop a script for the children. Get them to imagine being in the situation and practising what they will say. Role play the situation before practising in a real context.

Specific ideas

1. Use a Star Chart to record successes and earn rewards.
2. Develop a personal success album.
3. Produce a Special Treasure chest, with examples of special events, memories, successes.
4. Create situations where children cannot help but succeed.
5. Build on children's existing strengths.
6. Give them hugs.
7. Ask your children to imagine a special happy place. Ask them to draw/write about it. Practise this for gentle relaxation and self control.
8. Ask the children to write or draw a fairy tale, in which they are the hero/heroine and all ends well.
9. Ask your children to bury imaginary treasure (i.e. special qualities they possess). To get to it they have to cross a land where there are helps and hindrances. Each child makes a map illustrating where the treasure is buried and the problems to getting to it. How they get there can be a game in problem solving.
10. Your children write or draw about all the people that matter to them, and why they matter. This can show what needs they have and how they are fulfilled. A 'thank you' might also be employed.
11. The children draw a Self Portrait and write, in cartoon type bubbles, some of their unique qualities and skills.
12. Teach the children some positive evocative words that they can repeat throughout the day. For example, calm, strong, positive, happy, powerful.
13. Use a special pet name or term for the child, one that you never use for other children. This will add to its value because the child will learn that the name is special to them. Some examples could be, champ, buster, and so on.

When you do any of these or other strategies to build a child's self-esteem you are doing the right thing. You are beginning to make sure that the child is receiving some good mental health ingredients. It will take time for the child to show more confidence but you *must* not stop doing what is right. With some children your help may not produce the turn around you wish for. At such times your help may be all the more important in stopping them from 'falling' further.

New skills

Problem solving

For some children part of their low self-esteem is related to their inability to solve difficulties that they face. This can range from friendships to problems with their work. Here are two simple ideas that may help a child learn to think their situations through and take positive action.

(a) Stop Think Act. Giving some children clear directions for when they get stuck can help.
(b) What's the solution? What's the first step? If children can be helped to see what the solution is to a problem, they can be helped to break that down into small steps and begin with the first.

Positive thinking

The internal logic of having a low self-esteem is that a child's thinking will be negative. Like adults they will worry about things that never happen. Positive thinking involves teaching children to say certain positive, affirmative statements throughout their day; I can do this, I can cope with this, I am managing better than before. They can also be helped to complete and learn positive statements about themselves. Some examples:

(a) One thing I like about myself is

....

(b) Something I do well is

....

(c) A favourite memory I have is

....

(d) I look forward to

....

(e) I feel good when

....

Self control

Most children are able to control their behaviour internally, for some their behaviour seems to be externally controlled. This is especially true of children with low self-esteems. Children can be involved in learning skills of self control. They will need to know very precisely what the rules are and the behaviour that is expected of them as well as the consequences they will receive for following the rules. Depending on their age they may: record how often they do the behaviour; agree a contract to behave in particular ways for agreed rewards; rehearse their behaviour in a safe way, through drama.

Social skills

Having poor social skills will almost certainly lead to children having a poor self-esteem. Social 'know how' is about getting our needs met without causing problems to others. These are skills which can be learned.

Live modelling is when the children are told clearly the skill they need to practise and then watch other children carrying it out. Alternatively they could watch the skilled in action on a video or film.

Children may need to be coached to learn social skills. This would involve discussing the social skill, explaining its importance, for example politeness. They are given clear rules of when and how to use it. They can then practise it in a safe setting and receive feedback before they practise it in real settings.

A daily programme

The following elements have been found to raise self-esteem when used regularly: relax each day; have some exercise; include some good news; use uplifting music; smile through humour; set achievable targets.

The components of self-esteem

Self-esteem has three core components. We can use each of these to set up a range of activities that will strengthen each one. Many of these techniques you will already be using, the plan below will help you understand which aspect of self-esteem you are working on at any time.

COMPETENCY I CAN	VALUE I'M LIKED	CONTROL I WILL
TECHNIQUES What skills does the pupil have?	TECHNIQUES Have a 'special time' to be with them	TECHNIQUES Set learning targets with the pupil.
Involve them in recording their achievements.	Make time to let them show you what they want.	Involve them in taking responsibilities.
	Value their efforts as much as their achievements.	Let them choose rewards they have earned.
		Teach them self control strategies.

Section 2: Further notes on loss

Loss in the classroom

Accepting that loss is an experience that no child can avoid, we can try to build it in to our everyday teaching. The aim is not to prevent children experiencing the pain of loss or to unnecessarily create artificial situations for children to experience loss. What we can do is help children deal with their feelings in an open and caring context. We can show children that hurt feelings matter as much as broken bones. Some examples of loss can be addressed in the classroom.

Stories

Use stories such as *Badger's Parting Gift* to talk through loss issues at one remove from the children. This can allow them to express both their happy and sad feelings in a safe way.

Seasons

Use nature to explore the natural cycle of all living things. Children can grow plants and feed them with previously living material. They can experience how change is a positive and necessary process.

Class changes

Explore ways in which children can say good-bye to one another and those adults they have become attached to. Use photographs, letters and special gifts. An album of the changes they experiences will be treasured by all.

Friends

Help children to see the special qualities that all children have. Let them work in groups to get to know one another, ask how they will wish to say good-bye to children who leave their class.

Support

Support the children in understanding that we all hurt at some time; that tears are normal reactions and need not make us feel embarrassed or guilty; that big boys do cry. Discuss ideas for support on sad days.

Pets

Create special days when all pets are remembered. Children can talk about their memories, tell favourite stories, draw pictures. Have adults talk about the pets they have loved and cared for.

Music

Use the music of the day and classical music to explore the feelings that music produces in us. Let the children make music to express the different feelings that they have.

Loved objects

Allow special days when children can bring in their cherished toys. Have special class toys which carry certain memories of the class that can go home with children. Let the children make class 'toys'.

Poetry

Children can express through poetry the different feelings that they have towards themselves, others and their world. Poems to say good-bye or thank you can be read on special days.

Parental information

Schools will often be asked by concerned parents how best can they support their children through a family break-up.

Information

Make sure that children have brief, clear information. It is better that they are coping with an unpleasant reality than dealing with uncertainty. Make sure you explain matters to them often; like all of us they will not readily hear what they do not want to hear. Be careful to listen to what they are asking you before jumping in to answer questions that they haven't asked.

Worries

Children will have many worries at this time. They can worry that the remaining parent may also leave. Or they may be concerned as to whether they are going to change homes; or who will cut their sandwiches and can they keep their pet. Make time to be with them. They may often not wish to talk, that's okay. You may comment on their body messages, 'You look glum today.' Whatever you do, be sensitive to their worries. Remember children usually would prefer to have two parents.

Needs

Try to be flexible in the arrangements you make. Just like adults, children's needs will change over time. They may wish to attend an after school club and not come straight home.

Rights

Encourage your children to express their opinions. This does not mean doing what they want but it does allow you to take their views into account. Children have rights to safety, love, education, health care and play.

Responsibilities

Because your children are not able to care for themselves make their needs paramount. They are not possessions to be argued and fought over. They have no choice or control over what happens to them. Children can blame themselves for family break-ups. Help them to learn their boundaries of responsibility and that they were not to blame. Separation is an adult solution to adult difficulties.

Differences

Be the sort of parent you are. Children can adapt to the different home styles. You will be more effective and happy if you parent as you want to not as you think others expect you to.

Things to avoid

Arguments in front of children enlisting children to take sides; becoming over-possessive of your children; treating children as little adults; trying to be perfect; being emotionally blackmailed.

Remember

Even though it may not be easy, maintain a life for yourself.

References

Adair J. (1988) *Effective Leadership*. London: Pan Books.

Anthony M. (1981) 'An inside view of shared leadership'. *Educational Leadership* **38**, 6.

Attwood T. (1998) *Asperger Syndrome: A Guide for Parents and Professionals*. London: Jessica Kingsley.

Aubrey C. (1988) 'Organisational school psychology and school consultancy'. In Jones N. and Sayer J. (eds) *Management and the Psychology of Schools*. Lewes: Falmer Press.

Baldwin B. (1978) 'A paradigm for the classification of emotional crises', quoted in Maher C. and Zins J. (eds) (1987) *Psychoeducational Interventions*. Oxford: Pergamon Press.

Barber M. (1996) "Creating a framework for success inurban areas" in *Raising Educational Standards in the Inner Cities: Practical Initiatives in Action* eds Barber M. and Dann R., London: Cassel.

Belbin R.M. (1981) *Management Teams: Why They Succeed or Fail*. Oxford: Butterworth Heinemann.

Belbin R.M. (1993) *Team Roles at Work*. Oxford: Butterworth Heineman.

Bennathan M. and Boxall M. (1996) *Effective Intervention in Primary Schools: Nurture Groups*. London: David Fulton Publishers.

Blum M. and Naylor J. (1968) *Industrial Psychology Theoretical and Social Foundations*. Revised edn. New York: Harper & Row Publishers.

Bovair K. (1996) 'An abandoned state'. SPECIAL Spring '96 Cambridge: Hobsons.

Bowring-Carr and West-Burnham (1997) *Effective Learning in Schools*. London: Pitman Publishing.

British Psychological Society (1993) *Code of Conduct, Ethical Principles and Guidelines*. Leicester: BPS.

Brooks R. (1991) *The Self-Esteem Teacher*. American Guidance Service.

Burghes L. (1994) 'Lone parenthood and family disruption: the outcomes for children'. *Occasional Paper* 18, Family Policy Studies Centre.

Cabinet Office (1998) *Social Exclusion Unit Report Truancy and School Exclusions*. London: The Stationery Office.

Carvell F.J. (1980) *Human Relations in Business*. 3rd edition. London: Collier Macmillan.

Chess S., and Thomas, A. (1987) *Know Your Child*. New York: Prentice Hall.

Cockett M. and Tripp J. (1994) *Children Living in Re-ordered Families*. Joseph Rowntree Foundation.

Cornelius R.R. (1996) *The Science of Emotion: Research and Tradition in the Psychology of Emotion*. New York: Prentice Hall.

Coverdale G. M. (1973) 'Some determinants of teachers morale in Australia'. *Educational Research* 16, 1, 34–39.

Cummings and Davies (1994) *Children and Marital Conflict*. Hove: The Guilford Press.

Curry M. and Bromfield C. (1997) *Personal and Social Education for Primary Schools through Circle Time*. Tamworth: NASEN.

Davie and Galloway (Eds) (1996) *Listening to Children in Education*. London: David Fulton Publishers.

Deiro J. (1996) *Teaching with Heart*. Corwin Press, Inc.

Department of Education and Science (DES) (1989) *Discipline in Schools* (A Report of the Committee of Enquiry Chaired by Lord Elton). London: HMSO.

Department of Education and Science (1994). *Education of Children with Emotional and Behavioural Difficulties*. DES Circular 9/94. London: HMSO.

Department of Education (1994) *Code of Practice on the Identification and Assessment of Special Educational Needs*. London, COI.

DfEE (1997) *Excellence for All Children: Meeting Special Educational Needs*. London: The Stationery Office.

DfEE (1998a) *Meeting Special Educational Needs: A Programme of Action*. London: The Stationery Office.

DfEE (1998b) *Behaviour Support Plans* (Circular No 1/1998). London: The Stationery Office.

DfEE (1998c) *The Use of Force to Control or Retrain Pupils* Circular 10/98 London: The Stationery Office.

Durkheim E. (1952) *Suicide: A Study in Sociology*. London: Routledge and Kegan Paul.

Catherine Fenwick (1996) *Healing With Humour* http://saskweb.com/healinghumour/about.html

Fogell J.A. (1994) *The management of teacher morale in primary schools: An investigation into the social construction of the concept of teacher morale*. Unpublished MSc Research Report, University of London Institute of Education.

Fogell J.A. (1996) 'From strength to strength' *SPECIAL!* Summer 1996. Cambridge: Hobsons.

Fogell J.A. and Long R. (1996) *Spotlight on Special Educational Needs: Emotional and Behavioural Difficulties*. Tamworth: NASEN.

Fontana D. (1995) *Psychology for Teachers* 3rd Edition. London: Macmillan/BPS Books.

Furman B. (1999) *It's Never Too Late to have a Happy Childhood*. London: BT Press.

Galloway, Rogers, Armstrong and Leo (1998) *Motivating the Difficult to Teach*. Harlow: Longman.

Gazzangia M.S. (1992) *Selection Theory*. Harmondsworth: Penguin.

George E., Iveson C., Ratner H. (1990) *Problem to Solution: Brief Therapy with Individuals and Families*. London: BT Press.

Godfrey R. and Parsons C. (1998) *Report on Follow-up Survey of Permanent Exclusions from Schools in England – 1996/9*. Canterterbury: Christ Church College, ATL.

Goleman D. (1996) *Emotional Intelligence: Why it can matter more than IQ*. London: Bloomsbury.

Greenhalgh P. (1994) *Emotional Growth and Learning*. London: Routledge.

Gross R. (1992) *Psychology: The Science of Mind and Behaviour*. London: Hodder and Stoughton.

Grove A.S. (1987) 'Decisions decisions'. In Organ D. (ed.) *The Applied Psychology of Work Behaviour* 3rd edn, Plano Texas: Business Publications.

Hamblett J. (1991) Organisational climate: perspectives on a problematic concept. Unpublished PhD Thesis, University of London Institute of Education.

Herbert M. (1991) *Clinical Child Psychology Social Learning Development and Behaviour*. Chichester: Wiley.

Herzberg F. (1968) *Work and the Nature of Man*. London: Crosby Lockwood and Staples.

Hick H. and Gullett C. (1981) *Management*. London: McGraw Hill.

Hunshelwood R.D. (1987) *What Happens in Groups: Psychoanalysis, The Individual and The Community*. London: Free Association Books.

IAC. (1988) *The Report from the Interim Advisory Committee on Teachers' Pay and Conditions*. London: HMSO.

Jewett C. (1982) *Helping Children Cope with Separation and Loss*. London: B.T. Batsford Ltd.

Kanter R.M. (1987) 'Power'. In Organ D. (ed). *The Applied Psychology of Work Behaviour* 3rd edition. Texas: Business Publications, Plano.

Kutnick P. (1988) *Relationships in the Primary School Classroom*. London: Paul Chapman Publishing Ltd.

LeDoux J. (1998) *The Emotional Brain*. London: Weidenfeld and Nicolson.

Leseho J. and Howard-Rose D. (1994) *Anger in the Classroom*. Detselig Enterprises Ltd.

Lethem J. (1994) *Moved to Tears. Moved to Action: Solution Focused Brief Therapy with Women and Children*. London: BT Press.

Lewis M. and Samari C. (eds) (1985) *The Socialisation of Emotions*. New York: Plenum Press.

Magoon R.A. and Linkous S.W. (1979) 'The Principal and Effective Staff Morale' *NASSP-Bulletin* 63, 427, 20–28.

NHS Health Advisory Service (1995) *Child and Adolescent Mental Health Service, Together we Stand*. London: HMSO.

O'Connell B. (1999) *Solution Focused Therapy*. London: Sage.

Office for Standards in Education (1997) *Exclusions from Secondary Schools (1995–6)*. London: The Stationery Office.

O'Rourke, K. and Worzbyt, J. (1996) "Support groups for children". *Accelerated Development*.

Ostell A., Baverstock S. and Wright P. (1999) 'Interpersonal Skills: of managing emotions at work'. *The Psychologist* Vol 12, 1, 30–34.

Parris M. (1997) *Read My Lips: A treasury of the things politicians wish they hadn't said*. London: Penguin.

Raybould E. and Solity J. (1982) 'Teaching With Precision, Special Education'. *Forward Trends* Vol 9, 2, 9–13, NCSE, Stratford.

Rhodes J. (1993) 'The Use of Solution-Focused Brief Therapy in Schools'. *Education Psychology in Practice*. 9(1), 27–34.

Rhodes J. and Ajmal Y. (1995) *Solution Focused Thinking Schools*. London: BT Press.

Rice F.P. (1995) *Human Development: A Lifespan Approach*. 2nd edition. New York: Prentice Hall.

Rodgers B. and Pryor J. (1998) *Divorce and Separation: The Outcomes for Children*. York: Joseph Rowntree Foundation.

Roffey S., Tarrant T. and Majors K. (1994) *Young Friends: Schools and Friendship*. London: Cassell.

Rolls E.T. (1990) "A theory of emotion, and its application to understanding the neural basis of emotion". in: *Psychobiological Aspects of Relationships Between Emotion and Cognition: Special Issue of Cognition and Emotion*. Washington: Psychology Press.

Rutter, M. *et al.* (1979) *Fifteen Thousand Hours; Secondary Schools and Their Effects on Children*. Open Books.

Schmidt, T. (1993) 'Anger Management and Violence Prevention' a group activities manual for middle and high school students. Johnson Insitute.

Seach D. (1999) *Autistic Spectrum Disorder: Positive Approaches to Teaching Children with ASD*. Tamworth: NASEN.

Senge P.M. (1990) *The Fifth Discipline: The Art and Practice of the Learning Organisation*. London: Century Business Press.

Shaver P., Schwartz J., Kirson D. and O'Connor C. (1987) 'Emotion Knowledge'. *Journal of Personality and Social Psychology* Vol 52. Washington: American Psychological Association.

Sheldon B. (1995) *Cognitive Behavioural Therapy: Research, Practice and Philosophy*. London: Routledge.

Smith K.R. (1966) 'A proposed model for the investigation of teacher morale'. *The Journal of Educational Administration* 4, 2, 143–148.

Smith K.R. (1976) 'Morale: a refinement of stogdill's model'. *The Journal of Educational Administration* 14, 1, 87–93.

Smith P., Cowie H. and Blades M. (1998) *Understanding Children's Development*. 3rd edition. Oxford: Blackwell.

Smith R. (1998) *No Lessons Learnt: A Survey of School Exclusions*. London: The Children's Society.

Snyder, McDermott, Cook and Rapoff (1997) *Hope for the Journey*. Westview Press.

Sommers-Flanagan J. and Sommers-Flanagan R. (1997) *Tough Kids, Cool Counselling*. American Counselling Association.

Strongman K.T. (1996) *The Psychology of Emotion: Theories of Emotion in Perspective* 4th edition. Chichester: John Wiley.

Strayhorn, J., (1998) *The Competent Child*. The Guildford Press.

Stringer B. and Mall M. (1999) *A Solution Focused Approach to Anger Mangement with Children*. Questions Publishing.

Talmon M. (1990) *Single Session Therapy: Maximising the Effect of the First (and often only) Therapeutic Encounter* USA: Jossey-Bass.

Williams D.I. (1994) 'Is Competence Enough?' in 'Competent to Practise', *Educational and Child Psychology* 11, 1, 6–8.

Wilson T., Foley K. and Fleury B. (1990) *Goodwill Under Stress: Morale in UK Universities*. London: Association of University Teachers.

Wing L. (1996) *Autistic Spectrum Disorder*. London: Constable.

Wolman B. (1973) *Dictionary of Behavioural Science*. New York: Van Nostrum Reinhold.

Yule W. (1991) 'Work with Children Following Disasters', in Herbert M. (ed.) *Clinical Child Psychology: Social Learning Development and Behaviour*. Chichester: Wiley.

Index